AN INTRODUCTION TO
FRENCH CHURCH ARCHITECTURE

An Introduction to
FRENCH CHURCH ARCHITECTURE

by

ARTHUR GARDNER
M.A., F.S.A.

Author of *Medieval Sculpture in France;*
A Handbook of Medieval Sculpture in England

CAMBRIDGE
at the University Press
1938

CAMBRIDGE UNIVERSITY PRESS
Cambridge, New York, Melbourne, Madrid, Cape Town,
Singapore, São Paulo, Delhi, Mexico City

Cambridge University Press
The Edinburgh Building, Cambridge CB2 8RU, UK

Published in the United States of America by Cambridge University Press, New York

www.cambridge.org
Information on this title: www.cambridge.org/9781107646353

© Cambridge University Press 1938

First published 1938
First paperback edition 2013

A catalogue record for this publication is available from the British Library

ISBN 978-1-107-64635-3 Paperback

PREFACE

This book is intended to be a companion volume to my father's *Guide to English Gothic Architecture*, which seems to have supplied a want on the part of that section of the public which takes an intelligent interest in the memorials of the past among which it moves, but has not the time or opportunity to indulge in a prolonged or intensive study of the subject. My aim, therefore, is not to put forward new or attractive theories or to claim any merit for the book as an organ of original research, but to sum up as briefly and clearly as possible the outlines of the study, and to call attention to those features which will appeal to the eye of the tourist, with some explanation of their growth and development. The same plan has been adopted as in my father's book, and the descriptive text has been confined to a short introduction, followed by a large number of illustrations selected and arranged in such a way as to show the history and course of development, and accompanied by notes calling attention to the special points they are intended to enforce.

It is hoped that the book will prove a useful introduction for beginners to a fascinating study, and if any expert should be tempted by the pictures to invest in it I hope he will not condemn it for the absence of more advanced criticism, or for the presence of simple descriptions of what to him are commonplaces.

Keeping this object in view, plans, sections and diagrams have been kept to a minimum, and other technical matter requiring elaborate explanation has been excluded. The object throughout has been rather to stimulate interest than to provide advanced instruction, and to tempt readers to follow up the study by turning to more comprehensive works. A brief select bibliography including the most useful books available has been added.

In the notes I have attempted, perhaps rashly, to give as many dates as possible, but those for the earlier periods especially have been the subject of much controversy, and all that I can do here is to give such as seem best authenticated or most probable. It is impossible in a brief summary like this to give all the arguments and references consulted.

At the end of several sections I have added notes of additional examples not included in the text or illustrations. These lists of course are by no means exhaustive, and there are dozens of churches all over France which may have an equal claim to mention. The ground covered is so vast that extra examples seemed wanted, but it seemed better to put them as brief notes instead of cumbering the text.

Village churches, castles and domestic architecture should all be dealt with in a complete account, but I have had to keep the subject within bounds and a line has to be drawn somewhere.

A number of line drawings and plans have been reproduced from Sir Thomas Jackson's *Byzantine and Romanesque Architecture* and his *Gothic Architecture* by kind permission of his executor and the Cambridge University Press. Plate 138 is from a photograph by the late Mr Samuel Gardner. The rest are from my own negatives.

A. G.

February, 1938

CONTENTS

Map showing places illustrated in the Plates

Chapter I

BEGINNINGS

The story of medieval church architecture in France falls into three main divisions: (1) Romanesque, (2) Gothic, (3) Flamboyant. The term Gothic is usually employed to cover both (2) and (3), but it is difficult to find a single generally accepted title for the central phase. Certain subdivisions are also necessary, as, for example, a primitive period of experiment and revival before the full-blown Romanesque style got into its stride, and a transitional period while Romanesque was developing into Gothic. It is sometimes the fashion to divide Gothic into First and Second Pointed or Lancet and Geometric (French "Rayonnant"), but there is no great break between the two, and it will be simpler to take them together. The Flamboyant style comes in very suddenly, with much fewer transitional features than are found between our English styles of Early English and Decorated, or Decorated and Perpendicular, if we may still use the old-fashioned terms.

If for convenience the present survey is confined to the territories comprised by modern France, it must be realised that it was only towards the close of the medieval period that the boundaries approached at all to those established to-day. In the twelfth century France proper was a comparatively small domain round Paris, English kings owned most of the western half of the country, and even as late as the fourteenth century Bayonne was an English rather than a French town. Toulouse, Provence, Navarre, Burgundy were all practically independent states with constantly changing boundaries, and even the Pyrenees did not become a boundary until well on in our period, and there is little or no division in style between the early churches on both sides of the border in the west in Navarre, or at the eastern extremity in Roussillon and Catalonia. There was, indeed, more difference in race and language between the Frankish population of the north and the composite races of Southern France than between the latter and the Christian communities which were holding the fort against the Moors beyond the Pyrenees.

Another difficulty which the student of early French architecture has to face is the absence of any real agreement as to chronology. Monuments which can be certainly dated before the year 1000 are scarce, and even when records of consecrations or building still exist it is not easy to identify what is described with what remains, or to be sure that there has not been a subsequent rebuilding. In a brief treatise like this it will not be possible to discuss the conflicting theories in any detail, and all that can be attempted is to give a rough general idea of the position, leaving the study of details and more controversial issues to more ambitious publications.

THE MEROVINGIAN PERIOD

Buildings of the earliest days of the Church in Gaul are exceedingly scarce, though the writings of such men as Gregory of Tours prove that they existed. Many churches, no doubt, were of wood, and even the more important examples were probably of very simple design inspired by the aisled basilicas of Rome and the East and covered by wooden roofs. Decoration was mostly left to wall paintings and sculpture was confined to crude copies of Roman capitals. Such erections fell easy victims to the flames kindled by Norman and Saracen marauders.

The best-known building of this period is the so-called Temple Saint-Jean at Poitiers (pls. 1, 5a). This may have incorporated some remains of a Roman construction, and was to some extent remodelled at a later date, but the main portion with three apsidal recesses grouped round a central lantern tower appear to have formed a baptistery, the fourth side consisting of a later entrance porch. In the early days of the organized Church the rite of baptism could only be performed by a bishop, and considerable crowds assembled to meet him on his visits, necessitating special buildings, usually of a round or octagonal shape with a basin for immersion in the middle. By the ninth century, however, a ceremonial sprinkling seems to have been generally accepted, and fonts were provided in all churches at which the ordinary priest was allowed to officiate. Three or four[1] other such buildings exist in France, mostly in Provence, but with the possible exception of that at Venasque (pl. 2) may not be quite so old as the Poitiers example.

The crypts at Jouarre (pl. 3) and Grenoble are believed to go back to Merovingian times. They contain monolithic columns and capitals of a debased Roman type. The church of Saint-Pierre at Vienne, now used as a museum, is believed by de Lasteyrie to contain work of the fifth century in the outer walls decorated with columns and niched recesses, while the tall plain piers of the arcade and the apse are work of a tenth-century reconstruction (pl. 6).

THE CAROLINGIAN PERIOD

The reign of Charlemagne (768–814) brought an era of comparative prosperity, and the emperor's desire to emulate the splendours of ancient Rome led him to encourage building and the arts generally. His palace chapel at Aix-la-Chapelle (fig. 1) is of Byzantine design inspired by such a church as San Vitale at Ravenna. Its influence is seen in the centrally planned church of Germigny-des-Prés (pl. 4), near Orleans, in which four apses were grouped round a central space, covered by a cupola or tower. A short nave later replaced one of the apses, and the whole building has been so drastically restored as to render details suspect, but it still retains the original mosaic in the eastern apse. There are traces also of decorations and reliefs in stucco, a form of ornament which seems to have been in some favour at this time, though the friable nature of the material has prevented the survival of many examples. Some idea of what it was like may be obtained from the rich specimen at Cividale on the other side of the Alps.

[1] Aix, Fréjus, Riéz, Venasque.

The age of Charlemagne was, however, merely a temporary revival, and the disasters following the break-up of his empire, combined with the ravages of the Norman pirates in the tenth century, wiped out most of the evidences of what the ordinary architecture of his time was like. A few buildings dating from before the year 1000 have been identified, and must belong either to his time or have been reconstructed immediately after the ravages of the pirates. These are mostly of very simple design with aisles separated by plain unmoulded arches

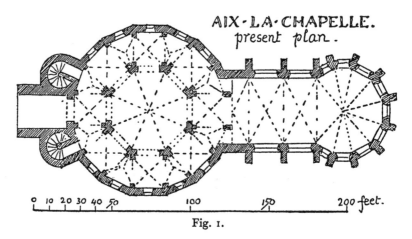

AIX-LA-CHAPELLE.
present plan.

o 10 20 30 40 50   100   150   200 feet.

Fig. 1.

resting on simple piers and lit by round-headed clerestory windows. Their chief feature is the decoration of the exterior walling by strings and patterns in coloured stones or bricks in the form of Roman tiles. Examples may be quoted at Saint-Generoux, Cravant (pl. 11) and Savennières (pl. 20a), and later in the Basse-Œuvre at Beauvais (987–98) (pl. 5b). Interlacing patterns, something like those on Saxon crosses in England, seem to have been the basis of their decorations, combined with stucco ornament and painting. In some of the later examples a kind of triforium gallery, or "tribune" as the French call it, seems to have been developed, as in the ruined church of Saint-Pierre adjoining the great abbey of Jumièges (pl. 12).

4

THE FIRST ROMANESQUE

A passage from the Cluniac historian Raoul Glaber written about 1047 has often been quoted. In it he tells how that once the ominous year 1000, in which men expected the end of the world, had been passed, a great movement began to restore and renew churches, and that all Christian peoples strove to emulate one another till it seemed that the world had "wished to apparel itself in a white robe of churches". The rapid increase in the skill of the builders under this stimulus led to the replacement of many of these early eleventh-century churches by lordlier structures within a few generations of their erection, making it difficult for us to appreciate the extent of the movement which excited Glaber's enthusiasm, but recently Señor Puig-i-Cadafalch has identified a large group of early churches belonging to the eleventh century, or thereabouts, and having common characteristics, which seem to represent the "white robe", and which he designated as "Le Premier Art Roman". These churches are found in all the countries bordering on the Gulf of Lyons, in Lombardy, Catalonia and Southern France, and extending up the Rhone Valley even as far as Switzerland. They are mostly small, though a few major examples exist, such as Ripoll to the south of the Pyrenees or Tournus in the Rhone Valley. They are usually built of small rough material and must have been whitewashed externally. Their most striking feature consists in flat pilaster buttresses dividing the outside walls, joined at the top by a cornice of two or more small arches. This has hitherto been regarded as a peculiarly Lombard feature, but Señor Puig has pointed out that these churches are as numerous in Catalonia as in Italy, though the type may have lingered longer in the latter country. He has traced over 100 churches in Southern France retaining some features of this movement.

The earlier churches were of a simple basilican plan, with aisles divided from the nave by plain round arches without mouldings, and

5

frequently supported by built-up piers lacking capitals. Windows were often double-splayed, with the glass in the middle of the wall, instead of on the outer edge as in later work. Churches usually ended at the east in an apse, and smaller flanking apses terminated the aisles. At first the apses alone were vaulted, the nave being covered by a wooden roof. Later, owing to the risk of fire, barrel-vaults were introduced in the more ambitious buildings, and in the next stage these were strengthened by transverse arches, and the plain square piers were reinforced to support them, thus assuming a cruciform section. In this we see features leading on to the complete Romanesque and Gothic schemes of the following centuries.

A late development is found in the addition of transepts with a cupola, or lantern tower, over the crossing. The earliest example of this is Saint-Vorles at Châtillon-sur-Seine, believed to have been built in 991 (pl. 7). Two remarkable churches of this series are to be found at Saint-Michel de Cuxa (consecrated 974 and enlarged 1020) and Saint-Martin de Canigou, both in Roussillon. They are in a ruinous condition,[1] but the former preserves a fine square tower decorated with the Lombard bands (pl. 102). This last feature is retained in churches like Saint-Aventin and Cruas, which are probably twelfth-century structures (pls. 95, 18). Orthodox French critics like Lefèvre-Pontalis classed these as belonging to a Lombardo-Rhenish school, deriving directly from Lombardy, and cite the record of William of Volpiano, an Italian trained at Cluny, who was called in to advise the builders of Saint-Benigne at Dijon (1001–17), and subsequently to reform abbeys in the north of France. Of this famous church at Dijon only the crypt remains, but a drawing made before its destruction gives some idea of its design (fig. 2). It consisted of a vast rotunda, the central space, possibly at first left open to the sky, being surrounded by a double ring of aisles in two stories, and the whole

[1] Saint-Martin de Canigou has in recent years been cleverly but drastically restored. Half at least of it must be regarded as a probable reconstruction rather than a genuine medieval monument.

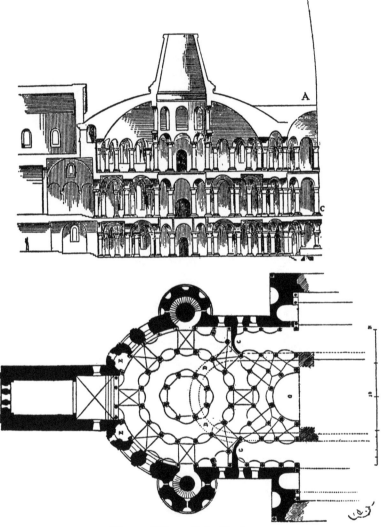

Fig. 2. Dijon—Saint-Benigne.

7

vaulted in stone. This remarkable church stands by itself, and can hardly be included in the series just described.

The largest, and most interesting, of these early churches in France is that at Tournus. There has been much controversy about its dates, but it was founded in the second half of the tenth century, and the body of St Philibert was placed in the completed crypt in 979. If, as

Fig. 3. Le Puy—Saint-Michel d'Aiguilhe.

is usually thought, the present crypt is that referred to in the records, it is an early example of the ambulatory plan with aisles round the curved apse and square-ended chapels opening out of it. The two-storied vaulted narthex, or western porch, is built up into a great tower, and is decorated externally with Lombard bands and cornices, as are also the walls of the nave. This part of the building appears to date from about 1000 and was consecrated in 1019. The nave has enormously tall round pillars of small stone and rubble construction, but the extraordinary vault, which will be described in the next chapter, is believed to have been added nearly 100 years later. The central part of the choir was reconstructed at the beginning of the twelfth century, though the outer part of the aisles and the projecting chapels may be of tenth-century date (pls. 13–16).

The little chapel of Saint-Michel d'Aiguilhe at Le Puy must surely occupy the most romantic situation of any church in the world (fig. 3; pl. 17). It was founded in 963, and the capitals of some of the columns certainly suggest a tenth-century date. The plan is irregular owing to the shape of the site, and the vaulting of a roughly groined type reminds one of some of the early crypts already mentioned. One walk, too, of the fine cathedral cloister at Le Puy has similar capitals and monolithic shafts shaped with Classical entasis, which features indicate a date not far from the year 1000 (pl. 10a).

The little Oratory of Saint-Trophime at Montmajour (pl. 8), opening into a rock-cut shrine, has sometimes been assigned to a very early date, but recent authorities do not think it earlier than the eleventh century in spite of its debased Classical capitals of distinctly Carolingian type.

Chapter II

ROMANESQUE

The latter part of the eleventh and first half or three-quarters of the twelfth centuries were marked by that great revival of art which we know as Romanesque. In it Western Europe, as it recovered from the barbarian invasions, took over the lead from the East, and developed new styles based on its own requirements and suited to its own environment. In its origin it was mainly a monastic movement, called into being by the demands of the monasteries, then at the height of their power and reputation, for nobler churches and more sumptuous buildings. We must, however, beware of the old misconception that we owe all these magnificent buildings to monastic craftsmen and monastic architects. Except perhaps in primitive times, when the monasteries were comparatively simple affairs, the work was done by lay masons and craftsmen. These may have been attached to the monastery by contract or otherwise, and the sacrist or some other monk may have been appointed as overseer or clerk of the works to do the business side of the work, to collect and pay the masons and to provide the materials, but the actual design and lay-out was the duty of the master-mason.[1] The abbot or bishop may have taken a great interest in the plans, but his part would not have been much more than that taken by a modern hospital or school council in stating their requirements to the architect. Such a specification as was sent from Cluny for the buildings of the new monastery at Farfa in Italy was no more than what could be laid down by an amateur patron, and the actual style in which it was to be carried out was left to the craftsmen on the spot. When, therefore, Viollet-le-Duc imagined a Cluniac style he was exaggerating the part taken by the monks. No

---

[1] For a further discussion of the position of the masons see chapter v.

10

doubt the influence of Cluny, which under its saintly abbots assumed the leadership of the monastic world, and sent out deputations to reform the old Benedictine abbeys all over Southern France and Spain, was very great. The monks knew what accommodation they wanted and the arts were in high estimation at Cluny, but an examination of the Cluniac priories shows that apart from the general lay-out each was built in the local style of the district in which it was set up.

The question of the origins of the Romanesque style cannot be treated adequately in a brief treatise like the present. Older writers regarded it as developed from the old traditions of Classical Roman art, gradually acquiring freedom from the canons of Vitruvius as the arch superseded the flat lintel. More recently it has come to be realised that the story is much more complicated, and other writers like Strzygowski have sought to belittle the influence of Rome and to trace everything back to the East, to Syria, Egypt and even Armenia and Mesopotamia. A living art, no doubt, drew inspiration from all available sources, whether from Roman ruins or from Constantinople which had remained all through the great centre of Christian civilisation, or even from hostile Moslem populations like the Moors in Spain, who brought with them a composite art learnt from the nations they had conquered in the Byzantine East in Syria and Egypt or farther away in Persia. But whatever the origins, it is obvious that the Western peoples built up at this period out of all these suggestions an art that was novel in itself, suited to new conditions, and containing the seeds of the still greater and more perfect Gothic art which was to follow it, and into which in its later phases it tended to merge.

Romanesque architecture may be studied from various standpoints, and it will be convenient to group our discussion first under five heads: (A) Plan, (B) Vaulting, (C) Articulation, (D) the Ornamental System, (E) Towers and Spires. Finally something must be said about the local schools.

(A) PLAN

The plan almost universally adopted for churches in the West was based on the basilica. This in its simplest form was an oblong building divided by rows of columns into a central nave flanked by two aisles. The wall above the columns was built up above the aisle-roofs and pierced with windows to light the central space, and the whole was covered with wooden roofs. It ended at the east in a rounded apse usually with a semi-spherical roof in stone or brick, and frequently smaller subsidiary apses were added on each side to end off the aisles. In larger churches, such as St Peter's at Rome, a projecting transverse bay, called a transept, was frequently added between the colonnaded portion and the apses which formed the sanctuary, thus producing a cruciform plan, which struck the imagination as a fit piece of symbolism. Besides the basilican plan there were also in the East numerous churches designed upon what is called a central plan. The main body of the building is enclosed by four great arches supporting a cupola. These were supported and prevented from falling outwards by surrounding apses or semidomes. Various elaborations were devised by grouping other domes round the central one. The most superb example of this type is Santa Sophia at Constantinople. This scheme was not adopted to any extent in the West, apart from such experiments as Charlemagne's chapel at Aix and Saint-Benigne at Dijon described in the previous chapter. In the eleventh century the abbey church at Charroux was built on to a rotunda rising to a tower, which alone survives (pl. 39). The little cemetery chapel at Montmajour (pl. 9) is centrally planned with a tower surrounded by four apses, the western one pierced to provide an entrance from the porch. This seems to have been consecrated in 1019. We have already mentioned the baptisteries built on this type of plan. It was also later on adopted in some of the churches built for the Knights Templars, in which case they were supposed to be modelled on the church of the Holy Sepulchre at Jerusalem. A few great churches like Saint-Front at Périgueux were built on this eastern plan, and will be described better in the section on vaulting, but although the centrally planned church was not often reproduced in the West its influence on the typical monastic church plan was of great importance. When the demand arose for stone-vaulted churches, a plan was evolved which seems to combine the basilican with the centrally planned scheme. If one of the latter churches is taken and a long basilican nave is substituted for its western

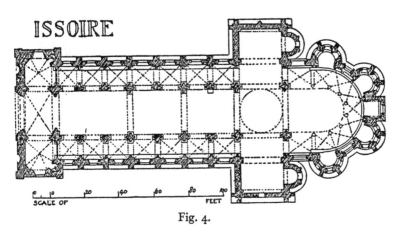

Fig. 4.

apse, the north and south apses produced to form transepts, the eastern apse pushed farther east by a vaulted presbytery, and the cupola built up to form a lantern tower, we have the typical Romanesque church of the twelfth century. Extra apsidal chapels could be added to the east of the transept and to the choir aisles, and western towers sometimes increased the dignity of the plan. Finally the aisles were carried round the apse, separated from the sanctuary by a circle of pillars, and chapels were opened up from the ambulatory thus formed. The church at Issoire may be taken as a typical example (fig. 4), while a more elaborate form with double aisles in the nave and aisled transepts may be found in the great church of Saint-Sernin, Toulouse

13

(fig. 5). These churches contain the elements on which the plans of nearly all the great cathedrals were based.

TOULOUSE S^T SERNIN

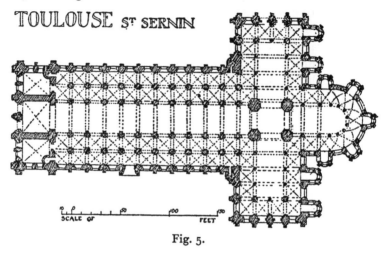

Fig. 5.

(B) Vaulting Scheme

This is probably the most important element in the formation and development of medieval architecture. The earlier churches had been mostly roofed with wood, but the numerous fires reported by the chroniclers, like that at Vézelay in 1120 in which 1127 persons lost their lives, produced a demand for a fire-proof method of covering in the churches. In the East, where timber was scarce, various forms of stone, concrete and brick vaulting had remained in practice since Roman times, and to these the Western masons turned for inspiration. Wooden roofs were retained for a time in the North, especially in Normandy, where good timber was available, but even there the more important churches usually received a stone vault later on. The engineering skill required to cover a wide space with a stone vault and the constructional devices required to support it led the masons on through an experimental period to the ultimate triumph of the vast Gothic cathedral.

Romanesque churches of the later eleventh and of the twelfth

14

centuries may be roughly classified by the system of vault adopted. Apart from the unvaulted wooden roofed basilica, three main types had been handed down from Roman times: (i) the barrel or tunnel vault, (ii) the groined vault, and (iii) the dome.

(i) *The Barrel Vault* is merely a simple continuous arch, like a tunnel. It has several disadvantages, the most important being the continuous outward thrust exercised by the stones composing it, which has to be met by enormously thick and heavy outer walls. This was partially met by throwing heavy transverse arches across the building which could be supported by thickening the wall to form buttresses at intervals, and it was also found that by making the shape pointed instead of round, part of the thrust could be directed downwards, where it was easier to meet. The pointed arch was known in the East from very early times, and was employed in Burgundy as early as the end of the eleventh century, as at Cluny. Until the middle of the twelfth century, however, it was mainly used for constructional features, while the round arch was employed for more ornamental forms. Bold attempts to raise a barrel vault over a lofty nave were made, especially in Burgundy and the Auvergne, the thrust being met by solid arches or half-arched vaults over the triforium, placed above the aisles, by means of which it was transferred to the outer walls. Many of these collapsed or needed reconstruction, like the nave roof of the great church at Cluny which fell in 1125, especially when an attempt was made to open clerestory windows above the aisle roofs, as had been done in the old wooden roofed basilicas. In the west country the difficulty was met by keeping the churches comparatively low, and raising the aisles to almost the same height as the central nave. The aisle vaults thus abutted the nave vault, and windows could be managed in the outer walls, leaving the central space to be lighted entirely from the aisles and a west window. These churches are usually very dark, though this is a lesser disadvantage in the south than in the less sunny north.

15

An interesting variety is found in the nave vault at Tournus, which consists of a series of short transverse barrel vaults supported on heavy arches across the building (pl. 15). This is satisfactory constructionally as each section resists the thrust of its neighbour, the two ends being abutted by the central and western heavy towers. It also leaves a space for high windows, but does not seem to have pleased aesthetically, as it was not repeated on a large scale, though often employed in the aisles by the Cistercians.

(ii) *Groined Vaults* are formed by the intersection of two tunnels, the sharp ridges where they intersect being termed groins. These are only satisfactory over a square space. The advantage of this type was that it concentrated the thrust at the corners of the square, making it easier to provide resistance at fixed points at intervals, and leaving a semicircular filling between these corners which was only a curtain wall easily pierced without danger to form windows. Groined vaults were most usually used to cover the aisles, but were sometimes also employed for the loftier central nave, as at Vézelay (pl. 64). If the nave was made twice the width of the aisles, one square in the centre corresponded to two at the sides, and this may have been one of the causes of the alternate bay system adopted in so many churches, where heavier and lighter piers succeed one another, the heavier carrying the transverse arches of the nave, and the lighter only those of the aisles. These, however, occur also in cases where no main vault was intended, and may then sometimes have been devised to support transverse arches on the top of which roof timbers could rest, as in some Italian churches like San Miniato at Florence, and possibly at Jumièges. The disadvantage of the groined type is that it requires an enormous amount of centring, or wooden temporary support on which it can be moulded during construction, and it was therefore difficult to construct over wide spaces, especially as medieval mortar had not the same strength as Roman cement. This objection also applies in a lesser degree to the barrel vault.

(iii) *The Dome.* In Persia, Mesopotamia and Syria we have seen, when discussing plans, that a system of domed or cupola vaulting had been devised owing to the lack of good timber. From these the centrally planned Byzantine churches had been derived, and their influence is seen in a remarkable group of churches in South-western France. The most striking of these is Saint-Front at Périgueux (fig. 6), a

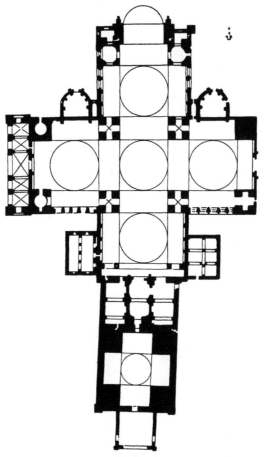

Fig. 6. Saint-Front, Périgueux (Viollet-le-Duc).

building consisting of a central dome surrounded by four others, which support it and bring the church to a cruciform shape, a porch and

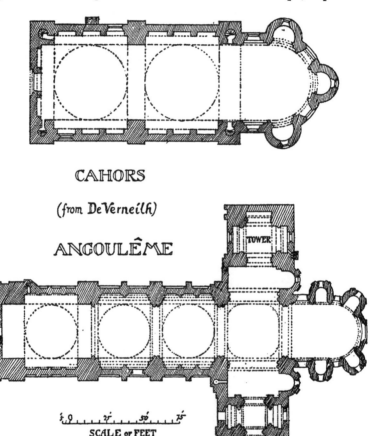

CAHORS

(from De Verneilh)

ANGOULÊME

Fig. 7.

tower being added at the west. The date of this has been the subject of controversy, but it is usually assumed that the plan was derived from that of St Mark's at Venice though it is now believed to be

18

considerably later than that famous church. In other cases the long western type of nave was retained, and was covered in by a series of domes, as at Cahors or Angoulême (fig. 7). A wide space was thus enclosed, and aisles were usually dispensed with. Among the most striking of these domed churches those at Solignac (pl. 41), Souillac, Le Puy and Fontevrault may be singled out for special mention.

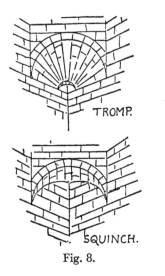

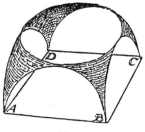

Fig. 8.   Fig. 9.

The chief problem in building a dome is to place a circular construction on the square formed by the four great supporting arches. One way of doing this was to construct little arches across the corners, thus converting the square into an octagon, whose wider angles could be more easily merged into the circle. These corner constructions are called tromps or squinches, and their shape can best be explained by the accompanying diagram (fig. 8). A better way was to build a solid ring over the four arches, and fill the corners between it and the arches by what are called pendentives, or spherical triangles with a double curve (fig. 9). On this circle a flattish cupola could be built up, only the central part requiring support during construction.

A curious experiment was made at Loches (pl. 43), where instead of cupolas the nave was roofed by a row of hollow spires—a northern version of a southern idea.

Finally, the western builders evolved a new system of their own in the *Ribbed Vault*, which superseded all the others, and after an experimental period developed what we know as Gothic style out of the Romanesque. Here again the question of origins is obscure. Some derive it from the ribbed domes of Armenia, others from a reinforcement of the groins by brickwork which did not project and was hidden by plaster—a method used occasionally by Roman builders—others consider it to have arisen spontaneously from underpinning the groins of an older vault, as was done in the crypt at Gloucester. Whatever the origin, it seems that the ribbed vault made its appearance in Lombardy and as far north as Durham before the end of the eleventh century, and a primitive example in the north tower at Bayeux is also claimed as belonging to the same date.

The advantage obtained by the use of ribs was great; intersecting arches could be built from the corners of the space to be covered on a comparatively narrow wooden centring, which could be removed for use elsewhere as soon as the keystones were inserted, and on this framework the filling could be easily contrived. At first, while the semicircular arch was in use, there was one difficulty owing to the fact that the enclosing and transverse arches were much shorter than the diagonals, causing the centre of the vault to rise to a domed shape, giving a wavy appearance over a series of bays. Attempts were made to get over this by stilting the transverse arches, and making the diagonals less than a semicircle, but this resulted in ribs springing at awkward and ugly angles from the capitals, as in the aisle of Saint-Étienne at Beauvais (pl. 29). The problem was further complicated if the wall rib, or "formeret" as it is called, had to occupy a space which did not allow the round arch to rise to the required height.

This trouble was met by the introduction of the pointed arch, which was much more flexible and could be adapted to any curve required. In the nave vault at Durham, completed by 1133, the transverse arches alone are pointed, and enable a level roof-line to be obtained. It is difficult to separate Norman work in England from that in Normandy itself, and it seems likely that this school played an important part in the development of the ribbed vault. It was, however, in the Ile-de-France that its full capabilities were completely worked out, a region which had curiously remained rather backward during the Romanesque period. Suger's rebuilding of the royal abbey of Saint-Denis, in the outskirts of Paris, is usually looked upon as the first complete example in which the ribbed vault, pointed arches and other features were combined to form the new style which we call Gothic, and which must be dealt with in a succeeding chapter.

(C) ARTICULATION

A great feature in medieval churches was the way in which the building was articulated. A harmonious effect is produced by giving each member of the constructive system its own work to do. Thus the piers of the nave of a vaulted church are usually of a cruciform section with semi-columns, or shafts attached on east and west sides to support the arches of the main arcade, and others on the north and south to support the vaulting ribs of nave and aisle. Vaulting shafts are carried from the ground to support the transverse arches of the vault, and where ribs are employed subsidiary shafts are often introduced below them. Another feature which produces a noble effect consists in the recessing of the arches, afterwards developed into the rich mouldings of Gothic buildings. This recessing had a purely practical origin, as it was first invented to save heavy centring during construction, just like the ribs of the vault. An arch of moderate thickness could be built on a narrow wooden framework, and when this was completed by the insertion of the keystone the stone arch itself could be used to serve as centring for a wider arch with stones projecting on each side of it to make up the necessary width. Further rows could be added if required, and then the square corners could be chamfered off or grooved to form mouldings to catch the light and give an appearance of richness and lightness to the work. Even the flat buttresses which thicken the walls of Romanesque churches, and serve to give variety to the external elevation, have their special work to do in strengthening the wall where the pressure of ribbed or groined vaults, or transverse arches is most felt, while ornamental cornices serve to bind the building together. All these features, which are characteristic of the great Gothic building, were evolved during the Romanesque period.

(D) The System of Ornament

As we have seen, the medieval church was first and foremost a practical construction. Its beauty and impressiveness was mainly derived from its suitability to its purpose and the rational way in which it met its requirements. Additional richness was also added by sculpture, but this was used with discretion. As a rule carving was not added to constructional features, but masks divisions in the articulation of the building such as capitals or string-courses. Doorways were frequently richly carved with many mouldings round their heads, and shafts on the jambs, while the tympanum, or filling of the door-head between the enclosing arch and flat lintel, provided a great field for sculpture.

Sculpture is too big a subject to be dealt with adequately in a brief treatise like this, and readers must be referred to special works on it. All that can be done here is to indicate roughly the manner in which it was employed, and to give one or two examples of the types of foliage favoured at the successive periods. This, however, may be best done when dealing with the local schools in the following section.

The *Cloister* formed the centre of the domestic side of the monastery, and was frequently very richly decorated, especially in the Cluniac priories, and the strange carvings of monsters, animals and grotesques called forth the famous protest of St Bernard, who prescribed a severe simplicity for his Cistercian foundations. The cloisters at Moissac, Elne and Arles are the most important (pls. 97, 99 and 87).

Towers also were a feature in which the medieval builder let his aesthetic ambitions outstrip the purely practical purpose for which they were erected. A tower had its special function as a place in which to hang the bells, and constructionally it performed a useful work as a solid mass to resist longitudinal pressure in a building, but it was often raised to a greater height than was purely necessary, and ornamented with arcading and openings and crowned with a pyramid or spire. A central or lantern tower usually replaced the cupola of Byzantine type over the crossing.

Windows at this time are almost invariably round-headed, and sometimes have shafts in the jambs. They are at times decorated with billet or zig-zag, especially in Normandy, and more elaborate scroll-work is common in the south-west. *Buttresses* are flat, and on the exterior of apses are frequently replaced by single or double shafts. Plain walls are often relieved by blank arcading, especially on the outside of the apse. The arches of the curved portion of the apse in churches with an ambulatory are often stilted and very narrow, and those of the main arcades are usually recessed in two orders, but the square profile is retained and rarely softened by mouldings until quite the end of the Romanesque period. Other features peculiar to certain districts will be referred to in the following sections.

(E) Towers and Spires

The early history of the bell-tower is obscure, but churches seem to have been provided with towers of some kind as early as the fifth century in the East. In France churches of the Carolingian period were provided with circular staircase-towers, and an old MS drawing of that at Saint-Riquier shows these as well as two round towers, one over the crossing and one at the west end.

In the eleventh and twelfth centuries towers are usually provided, but their position and number varies. The most usual position is over the crossing, where they are frequently raised over a cupola, especially in the south and east, or where they form a lantern-tower with windows illuminating the centre of the building, as in Normandy. A single western tower is less common than in England, but a tower at the west and another over the crossing, as at Saint-Aventin (pl. 95) or Cruas (pl. 18), is frequent. In central districts a large western tower spreads over the whole front and forms a vast porch, sometimes with small turrets at the side, as at Saint-Junien (pl. 108b) or in the magnificent but incomplete example at Saint-Benoît-sur-Loire (pl. 33), where it seems to have formed a kind of monastic fortress-keep with a large upper chamber over the porch comparatively safe from attack. The same requirement may explain the great tower at Tournus (pl. 13) which has mere slits for windows. A central and two western towers was the scheme most favoured by monastic churches in Burgundy and the north, as at Paray-le-Monial (pl. 65) and Caen (pl. 28) or Bayeux (pl. 103). Cluny had no less than seven, one over the main crossing, flanked by one over each transept, two at the west end, one over the crossing of the second transept, and a little-bell tower next the main south transept. Single towers were often placed at the side either of nave or choir, as at Saint-Léonard (pl. 109b), or Cunault (pl. 107a). In the north-east twin towers sometimes flank the apse, as at Morienval (pl. 105b), a feature which links such churches with those of the Rhineland where it is very common.

Towers may be either square or octagonal or round, or combine these shapes in various stages. The square tower may be illustrated by the early example at Saint-Michel de Cuxa (pl. 102), or that of Saint-Trophime at Arles (pl. 106a) which carries on eleventh-century features into the twelfth. These southern towers end in a platform and are merely crenellated at the top or covered with a low roof. Square towers over the crossing, crowned with low stone spires, may be represented by that at Saint-Rambert (pl. 105a). Openings are grouped, most frequently in twos, and blank arcading is frequently employed, early examples in the south sometimes having the Lombard bands, as at Cuxa (pl. 102).

Round towers are not common after the early period, but fine Romanesque examples occur at Uzés and Cruas (pl. 18). Octagonal towers are favoured in Burgundy, as at Anzy-le-Duc (pl. 106b), which might not look out of place in Italy, and in the Auvergne, where they are placed over an oblong stage raised over the transept.

In Poitou a round stage is placed over a square and crowned with a conical spire faced with a kind of stone scale ornament, as at Saintes, Périgueux and Poitiers (pl. 108a).

The early tower at Brantôme (pl. 104) introduces another type, built in receding stages with lofty gables over arches in the middle stage, serving to distribute the weight on to the stronger corners. These lofty gables were used later to mask the transition from the square to the octagonal upper stages in preparation for a lofty spire, and may be regarded as the ancestors of the splendid scheme of the south-western spire of Chartres (pl. 180) or the graceful thirteenth century example at Senlis (pl. 193a). A fine intermediate example may be found at Saint-Léonard, near Limoges (pl. 109b).

The transition from square to octagon at the base of the spire, or the stage below it, was managed inside by squinches, or little arches across the corners, and to prevent these spreading the corners were weighted with pinnacles, as at Déols (pl. 109a) or Saint-Germain at Auxerre (pl. 110a). A modified form of this type was used in the transitional spire at Vendôme (pl. 110b), where the gables are used in conjunction with the pinnacles, and this led to very effective combinations in the next century, as at Caen (pl. 25) or Bayeux (pl. 103), where later spires were added to the Romanesque towers.

M. Deshoulières, following Lefèvre-Pontalis, classifies the Romanesque churches of France as belonging to nine local schools. The boundaries of these are rather vague, and overlap in places, and some are much more distinctive than others. It is only possible here to pick out a few of the most characteristic local features.

These nine schools are: (1) Ile-de-France and Champagne, (2) Normandy, (3) Lombardo-Rhenish, (4) the Lower Loire, (5) South-west and Poitou, (6) Auvergne, (7) Burgundy, (8) Provence, (9) Languedoc.

(1) ILE-DE-FRANCE AND CHAMPAGNE

This region, which took the lead later on, did not produce many important or distinctive churches. Few of them were originally vaulted, and the design was simple. Ambulatories and triforium galleries were rare, and the ornament was much influenced by Normandy. No doubt many characteristic examples were swept away to be replaced by fine Gothic churches when the new style came into fashion. The church of Saint-Rémi at Reims is the most important early example; this dated from the first half of the eleventh century, but was much altered *c.* 1170, when an early Gothic vault and apse were planned. It was badly damaged in 1918 (pl. 21).

Saint-Étienne de Beauvais has a fine twelfth-century nave, and contains some early ribbed vaults (pl. 29).

The church at Vignory is an interesting early example (pl. 23) with low unmoulded arcades surmounted by a kind of triforium of ponderous design and covered by a wooden roof. The nave at Montier-en-Der is of a very similar type (pl. 22). These last are on the south-eastern fringe of this district, but belong to the northern rather than southern types.

Other examples:

Saint-Loup de Naud. Mid-twelfth century. Fine porch with sculpture of late twelfth century.

Paris. Saint-Germain-des-Prés. Begun in eleventh century. Nave early twelfth century. Choir probably consecrated 1163. Has some very early flying buttresses. Badly and excessively damaged and restored.

Lillers. First half of twelfth century. Wooden roof. Pointed main arcade, but rest round-arched.

(2) NORMANDY

This province played an important part from the eleventh century onwards. Famous builders like William of Volpiano and Lanfranc have been cited as having introduced the style from Lombardy, but apart from a preference for the alternate bay scheme and for large triforium galleries, or "tribunes" as the French call them, there are few Lombard features. Bernay was begun early in the eleventh century (pl. 19a) and the great abbey of Jumièges dates from 1040 to 1067 (pl. 24). Much of the enterprise and energy of the Normans was diverted into England after 1066, and the vast abbey churches built by the Benedictines there with the encouragement of William the Conqueror were on an even larger scale than those in Normandy itself. These huge churches were not originally designed for vaults over the nave, though groined vaults were sometimes provided over the aisles, and ribbed vaults were added late in the twelfth century to such churches as Saint-Étienne (or the Abbaye aux Hommes) at Caen. Ambulatories were rare, roomy tribunes were provided over the aisles, and lantern towers over the crossing were favoured, as well as western towers, and pave the way for the grand transitional and thirteenth-century steeples for which Normandy is famous. All arches and windows are round-headed, and exteriors are severe and plain, though in later examples, and to a greater extent in England, wall arcades, sometimes with intersecting arches, are favoured. In later examples chevron or zig-zag, billet, key-pattern and other rough and rather barbarous ornaments give a rich effect round doors or windows, or the arches of the main arcade, as at Bayeux (pl. 30), but figure-sculpture is rare and very primitive.

Other examples: Normandy.

Cerisy-la-Forêt. Second quarter twelfth century. Fine cruciform church with unaisled apse. West end destroyed. Has transverse arches across nave to support timbers of a wooden roof.

Mont-Saint-Michel. Abbey church begun late eleventh century, and considerably altered after a fire in 1112. Choir rebuilt *c.* 1450. Fine cloister of thirteenth century.

Caen. Saint-Nicholas. Desecrated and now difficult to obtain admission. Consecrated 1093. Wood roof, aisles groin-vaulted. The high roof over apse a striking feature of exterior.

Ouistreham. Nave *c.* 1160. Richly ornamented arcade. Sexpartite vault. Fine façade. Choir thirteenth century.

Creully. Nave mid-twelfth century. Sexpartite vault. Rich decoration of arcades.

Lessay. Finished *c.* 1130; and consecrated 1178, probably after the addition of the quadripartite vault.

Saint-Gabriel (Calvados). Fine fragment *c.* 1150. Tower, choir and transept survive. Richly carved arcades.

Sequeville-en-Bessin. Fine tower (with thirteenth-century spire) and nave restored after being burnt by Henry I of England in 1105.

(3) LOMBARDO-RHENISH

This is found along the eastern borders and extends into Alsace-Lorraine and Belgium. It is allied to what is found in Germany, whose influence is seen in the plan with an apse at each end found at Tournai, Verdun and Nevers (pl. 32). Here the old Carolingian traditions survive and Lombard bands and other features are commoner than farther west. We have already described the early churches which show this most strongly at Tournus and in Roussillon, in the previous chapter. The churches farther north are usually on a moderate scale, with round unmoulded arches and wooden roofs, and a Carolingian feature, much favoured later in Germany, is the placing of pairs of towers east of the crossing at the springing of the apse, as at Morienval (pl. 105 b).

Other examples:
Saint-Dié, Marmoutier, Beaume-les-Messieurs, Neuviller, Rosheim.

(4) THE LOWER LOIRE

This is a rather ill-defined school, covering a vast territory in Central France, and receiving influences from the surrounding districts. It contains, nevertheless, some very imposing churches, such as Saint-Genou (pl. 35), and the great abbey church of Saint-Benoît-sur-Loire (pl. 34) which follows the plan of Cluny in having double transepts, a rare feature in France. Massive columns and heavy, boldly carved, though somewhat rough, capitals produce an impression of grandeur and strength, as in the vast porch, carried up into a tower, which covers the whole west front at Saint-Benoît (pl. 33). There is frequently a long choir interposed between the crossing and the apse, covered with a barrel vault, and separated from the aisles by closely placed columns supporting small unmoulded arches. Tribunes are absent, but are replaced by a false triforium or wall arcade, as again at Saint-Benoît and Saint-Genou. We may hesitate as to whether we place the churches of the Limousin here or in the Languedoc school. The western porch towers of such churches as Saint-Léonard, Saint-Junien (pl. 108b), or La Souterraine, built in succeeding stages, form a distinct group, and some of the doorways are enclosed with lobed arches, possibly a suggestion from Moorish sources.

Other examples:
La Celle-Bruère. Eleventh-century barrel vaulted without clerestory.
Chateaumeillant. *c.* 1100. East end has seven apses. Aisles nearly as lofty as nave.
Neuvy-Saint-Sépulchre. Round church with heavy piers and arches. Founded 1045.
Fontgombault. Consecration 1141.
Le Dorat. Heavy porch tower at west something like that of Saint-Junien. Round lantern tower over crossing. Pointed arches. Unfinished in 1130. Nave second half of twelfth century.

Selles-sur-Cher. Sculptured frieze on exterior of apse chapels.

Saumur. The churches of Saint-Pierre and Notre-Dame de Nantilly date from the twelfth century, and the style is much affected by that of the south-western school.

Saint-Aignan. Fine twelfth-century church with eleventh-century crypt. Remarkable capitals.

(5) THE SOUTH-WEST

This is a large district extending from the mouth of the Loire as far as Bordeaux and even beyond, and extending its influence beyond its proper borders, for in such matters there is no defined boundary. The main centres from which the style radiated were Angoulême and Poitiers.

A number of the more important churches are covered by a series of domes, as described in our section on vaulting, but the most frequent scheme is a barrel vault, frequently pointed and strengthened by transverse arches, and it is thought that some of the domical vaults were adopted in the second half of the twelfth century to replace barrel vaults which had collapsed under the continuous thrust exerted by this form of construction. The barrel-vaulted churches are usually comparatively low, and the aisles narrow and lofty, the semicircular or quarter-circle vaults of the aisles being raised very high to abut the main vault and to allow the light from the aisle windows to enter the central nave, which in spite of this usually remained very dark, as the builders did not attempt to pierce their heavy vaults with clerestory windows. Where there are transepts the crossing is often surmounted by a lantern tower or a kind of dome supported on tromps or squinches (see p. 19), and apses are frequently surrounded by ambulatories separated from the sanctuary by narrow arches on tall columns.

But the most characteristic feature of this school is the lavish use of sculpture on the exterior. Façade and apse are covered with decoration and the astonishing richness of the sculpture makes up in quantity and picturesque effect for what it lacks in refinement and proportion. The façade is usually divided into three portions each containing a richly carved arch on the lowest story, only the centre one being in most cases pierced by a doorway. The tympanum in the head of the arch is seldom filled, and those which have carving are small and unimportant, but the orders of the arch over the door are extraordinarily elaborate, each voussoir being carved separately with a single subject.[1] The most famous of these façades may be found at Notre-Dame-la-Grande, Poitiers (pl. 44) and Angoulême (pl. 36), and one of the most imposing churches of this type is that at Aulnay de Saintonge. Here the transept front is as rich as the western and the apse windows are surrounded with carving (pls. 46–49).

Towers, as at Poitiers, are square with an upper arcaded portion round or octagonal, surmounted by a low stone spire covered with a scale decoration (pl. 108a).

Other examples:

Poitiers. *Sainte-Radegonde.* Choir 1083–1099. Nave thirteenth century. Fine west tower.

Poitiers. *Saint-Hilaire.* Consecrated 1059. Barrel vault built in 1130, when an interior arcade was added to reduce span. Fine group of apses. The eleventh-century church is attributed to an English master-mason.

Saint-Michel d'Entraigues. 1137. Octagonal church. Much restored in the nineteenth century.

Fontevrault. Vaulted with series of domes. Much restored. Contains effigies of Richard I, Henry I and queens of England. Consecrated 1119.

Saint-Jouin-de-Marne. Completed 1130. Fine façade, upper part restored.

Parthenay, Parthenay-le-Vieux, Ruffec, Chalais, Surgères, Bordeaux Sainte-Croix, Échillais, Échebrune, Maillezais, Écurat, Vouvant, Cognac, Fenioux, Chadennac (dated 1140), etc. are all remarkable for richly ornamented façades, and mostly seem to date from the second quarter of the twelfth century.

Rioux and *Retaud* are noted for the rich decoration of their apses.

Saint-Savin. Lofty columns. Barrel vault. No clerestory. Choir probably *c.* 1050, nave a little later. Famous for its early wall paintings.

Barsac. Fine tower.

---

[1] A remarkable instance of this occurs at Saintes, where the Massacre of the Innocents is carved in this position. As each soldier and each infant is allotted one voussoir, they are represented as the same size, which causes confusion and makes it difficult to identify the subject.

(6) AUVERGNE

The mountainous country round Clermont-Ferrand developed a peculiar style of its own. The dark volcanic stone of the district was used alternately with a whitish stone to form a kind of rough mosaic pattern to decorate cornices and gables. Towers are usually central and octagonal in shape, supported on squinches, and the transept rises in stages to support them, giving a high-shouldered effect which is peculiar to the district. The interiors are dark with a round barrel vault and a triforium gallery, or tribune, over the aisles

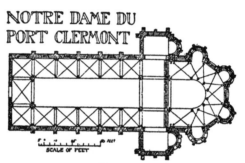

Fig. 10.

vaulted with a quarter-circular roof to abut the central span. Transverse strengthening arches are usually omitted, and there are window-like openings over the tower arches. The general effect is simple and archaic, but though excavations have revealed traces of a tenth-century ambulatory with radiating chapels under the present cathedral, which must have been one of the earliest examples of this plan, it is generally believed that none of the existing churches go back beyond the twelfth century, apart from crypts or auxiliary buildings like the narthex at Chamalières.

There is a tendency to provide doorways with a triangular-shaped lintel, and the capitals, especially those of the sanctuary are large and covered with sculptured scenes of exceptional interest.

Other examples:

These all seem to be of twelfth-century date. Notre-Dame du Port at Clermont is apparently one of the earliest of the type, Issoire and Mozac the latest. All are much of a type, and the general description given covers most of them.

Brioude, Chamalières, Volvic, Saint-Saturnin, Orcival, Menat, Chauriat (good example of colour mosaic on gables), *Riom, Mozac* (capitals).

Le Puy (stands rather apart from general group—vaulted by series of domes), Moorish influence is seen in some of its details.

(7) BURGUNDY

This province was of the greatest importance as it early became one of the chief centres of monasticism. Cluny was the centre from which radiated the chief vigour of the monastic orders during the eleventh and twelfth centuries, and played the chief part in that patronage of the arts which led to the great revival of architecture in Western Europe. As has been already pointed out, Viollet-le-Duc was mistaken in speaking of a Cluniac style, for though many monasteries were reformed under the auspices of Cluny, the actual buildings were in the local style of the province in which they were erected, and we must therefore only look to Cluny for a general inspiration and for the lofty enthusiasm for art which produced these great buildings.

Of the great church at Cluny, the largest hitherto erected in Europe, only one transept crowned by two minor towers remains (pl. 63a), but this fragment combined with the records enables us to form some idea of what it was like (fig. 11). Like Saint-Benoît-sur-Loire, and many English cathedrals, it had an eastern as well as the main transept, and was very lofty. Although begun in 1088 all the constructional arches seem to have been pointed, and the vault was of the pointed barrel type, the round arch being retained for ornamental features such as windows and doors. Later a narthex or western porch-extension was added. The nave was flanked by double aisles, and above the nave arcade was a double range of arcading with fluted pilasters, with windows in the high walls. This daring piercing of windows high

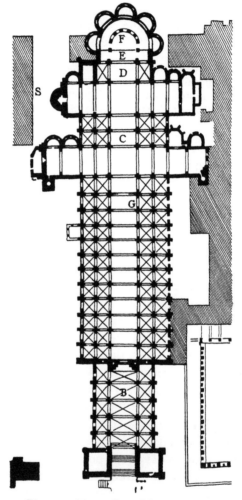

Fig. 11. Cluny (from Viollet-le-Duc).

34

up in a barrel-vaulted church was a feature of Burgundian construction, and not infrequently led to disaster. The church at Paray-le-Monial, built like the parent church at Cluny by the great abbot St Hugh, may serve to give an idea of the style of the latter (pls. 63 b, 65).

The fine early church of Saint-Étienne at Nevers (pl. 71) has a large triforium, or tribune, as well as a clerestory under a round barrel vault. It was erected in the second half of the eleventh century, and shows the enterprise of the builders of this early date who trusted to the solidity of the construction to counteract the risks of a somewhat dangerous design.

The features which distinguish the more important Burgundian churches are:

(1) Great height. (2) Barrel vaults, usually pointed and pierced with clerestory windows. (3) Employment of Classical details derived from Roman remains, such as fluted pilasters. (4) Vigorous and distinguished sculpture on doorways and capitals. (5) A narthex at the west end is frequent. (6) Aisles usually groin-vaulted.

The employment of fluted pilasters can be well seen at Autun, a cathedral built under a Cluniac bishop, and the arcading or false triforium over the main arcade (pl. 68 b) is almost a replica of the upper story of the Roman gate of that city, though similar features had already appeared at Cluny some years before. The cathedral at Vienne and other churches display similar features, while the fluted pilasters continued in use into the second half of the twelfth century, as in the almost transitional church at Saint-Menoux (pl. 76).

The sculpture on capitals at Cluny (now in the museum there), Vézelay, Autun, Saulieu and elsewhere is remarkable both for its subjects and treatment, and large tympanum carvings over doorways are common. Foliage is very bold and skilful, and large rosettes, as at Vézelay and Avallon (pl. 74), are characteristic, as well as capably executed Corinthian capitals and Classical scrolls.

In default of Cluny the great church at Vézelay is perhaps the most striking building in the area. Here the arches are round and, like the transverse arches of the vault, are built in alternate courses of light

35   3-2

and dark coloured stone. There is no triforium and the nave has a groined vault, which permits of good upper lighting (pl. 64).

Western towers were built at Cluny, Vézelay and Paray-le-Monial (pl. 65).

The magnificence of the Cluniac and cathedral churches caused a reaction in favour of simplicity, led by the Cistercians who rejected sculpture, painting, stained glass and lofty towers, and whose buildings depend for effect on beauty of proportion and suitability for their purpose. The earliest surviving church of this order is at Fontenay and is a huge empty structure with a plain square east end, a pointed barrel vault with solid transverse arches, and capitals of the simplest description (pl. 77). There are no mouldings, triforium or clerestory, and the aisles are vaulted with a series of little transverse barrel vaults at right angles to the nave, a system transported by the Cistercians to our English Fountains. These were probably divided up into a series of side chapels to contain the numerous altars demanded by the ritual. There is a beautiful cloister at Fontenay (pl. 78) depending for its effect entirely on its proportions and general design and rejecting entirely the rich sculpture which added so much interest to the Benedictine and especially the Cluniac cloisters. The church was begun in 1139 and consecrated in 1147. The other great Cistercian church at Pontigny was not begun till c. 1150; it has a ribbed cross-vault and is well on the way to Gothic (pls. 128, 129).

Other examples:

> *Vienne.* Twelfth-century nave with fluted pilasters. Later choir and Flamboyant façade.
> *Avallon.* Simple pointed arches and pointed barrel vault, late twelfth century. Richly carved doorways (see pl. 74). The apse is the only part which could have been consecrated in 1106.
> *Charlieu.* Rich doorways and part of cloister. Rest ruinous.
> *Souvigny.* Large monastic church of early twelfth century, much altered and added to at various dates.
> *Langres.* Late twelfth century, with Renaissance façade.
> *Bois-Sainte-Marie.* Capitals.

(8) PROVENCE

The churches of this region are usually less imposing than those of Burgundy: they are often without aisles, and when they have them they are usually small and narrow. There is no triforium or tribune, and the barrel vaults are usually, though not without exception, pointed. A low dome on squinches is used to cover the crossing, and the apse is often decorated with ribs which rise to meet at the summit. It has been suggested that this feature, which occurs very early in Armenia, was one of the origins of the Gothic ribbed vault, but the apse ribs have more in common with the reinforcing transverse arches of the barrel vaults, and are usually built at the same time as the surrounding walls and even in the same stones, which fact makes the theory unacceptable. Roofs are flat and laid directly on the vaulting instead of having an outer cover of tiles or lead raised on a wooden framework as was required in the north to throw off the snow. Mouldings are almost entirely absent, and in the interior capitals are usually replaced by a simple narrow abacus.

Abundance of good building stone resulted in fine and solid masonry, and as usual in a southern climate windows are small and the buildings rather dark. Fluted pilasters are less frequent than in Burgundy, but are sometimes used as buttresses on the exterior of the apse, as at Cavaillon (pl. 84a), where the apse is polygonal outside though round within. Lombard bands and cornices sometimes give an appearance of greater antiquity than the actual date of the building, as at Cruas (pl. 18) or on the tower at Arles (pl. 106a).

The most remarkable feature in many of these churches, few of which can be dated earlier than the mid-twelfth century, is the skilful reproduction of Classical ornament, based on the numerous Roman remains still extant. Doorways, especially, placed under a kind of pediment supported by fluted or twisted columns, are richly carved with egg and dart and other Classical mouldings. Such doorways as those at Saint-Restitut (pl. 85), Saint-Gabriel (pl. 86) or Avignon would be quite in place on a real Roman monument, and some of them may even incorporate fragments from ancient buildings. Capitals of the Corinthian order are very well reproduced and bits of cornice are even introduced, as on the marvellous triple portal of Saint-Gilles (pl. 82). The figure-work here and at Arles and Romans is mainly based on Roman or Gallo-Roman sarcophagi of which numerous examples are preserved still in the museum at Arles.

A very beautiful series of cloisters survive, of which the most important are those at Arles (pl. 87), Vaison (pl. 89), Montmajour, Saint-Rémy and Aix. The last four have light bays of three or four arches enclosed in a heavy depressed arch, designed to give solidity to support the vaulting. Capitals finely carved with figure and foliage, and at Arles large figures and reliefs, give great beauty and richness to these cloisters, and contrast strongly with the austere and purely constructional ornament of the Cistercian cloister at Fontenay farther north (pl. 78).

Other examples:

> *Avignon.* Notre-Dame-des-Doms (Cathedral). Consecrated 1069, but little more than the core and plan of the original church remains. It was reconstructed in the twelfth century and is filled with clumsy Renaissance fittings. There is a Classical type west porch.
> *Carpentras.* Swags of fruit and flowers suspended from skulls of oxen in imitation of Classical carving.
> *Silvacane.* Abbey church.
> *Die.* Pointed barrel vault, very wide and low, with no aisles.
> *Cloisters* at Aix, Le Thoronet, Sénanque.

(9) LANGUEDOC

Under this head may be grouped the churches in the area between the Pyrenees and the *massif-central*, and in the valleys running up into the mountains, but excluding the extreme south-western district bordering on the Bay of Biscay, which belongs to the south-western school. Lefèvre-Pontalis included the churches of the Limousin, which have been here placed in no. 4, owing to the analogy between

38

their porch-towers and that of Saint-Benoît-sur-Loire, but other features might connect them equally with their southern neighbours.

Toulouse may be regarded as the chief centre, though the lack of building stone resulted in the development of a style of brick architecture which gives it a local flavour, as in the great church of Saint-Sernin (pl. 90). In plan and general design this church belongs to a group of great pilgrimage churches built during the second half of the eleventh century, and including that at Conques (pl. 93) and the far-away cathedral of Santiago de Compostela in Spain (pl. 92), for at this early date the Pyrenees do not seem to have formed a boundary between France and Spain which in their modern form had hardly come into existence. These churches have an ambulatory with chapels and a very long transept; there are spacious tribunes but no clerestory windows except in the apse, and round barrel vaults with transverse strengthening arches. Apart from the doorways the exteriors tend to be severe and plain. The destroyed church of Saint-Martial at Limoges seems to have been of this type, and it has been suggested that the whole group derived from Saint-Martin at Tours, of which hardly a trace survives.

Some of the domed churches, like that at Cahors, extend into this district, and the later churches tend towards a solidity and simplicity of design. The sculpture at Toulouse is of a heavy type which is found also in Northern Spain *c.* 1100, but at Moissac, Beaulieu, Cahors and Conques there are enormous tympanum carvings, which seem to connect them with the Burgundian schools. That at Conques belongs to the Toulouse-Santiago type, but the strange and contorted figures of Moissac, Beaulieu and Souillac have more in common with Burgundy.

The cloisters at Saint-Bertrand-de-Comminges (pl. 100) and Saint-Lizier (pl. 101) are very attractive, but that at Elne in Roussillon (pl. 99) has more in common with those of Provence. The famous reliefs and capitals in those at Moissac date from 1100 (pls. 97, 98), and seem in the foliage to display Moorish influence. There is a great controversy between French and Spanish authorities as to the respective priority of Moissac and Santo-Domingo de Silos, near Burgos.

Other examples:

> *Carcassonne. Saint-Nazaire.* Solid barrel-vaulted nave *c.* 1095. Choir fourteenth century.
>
> *Valcabrère.* Small Pyrenean church of eleventh century, very solid, and parts may be older still. Interesting late twelfth-century porch with statues.
>
> *Bozouls.* Early twelfth-century church with apse and ambulatory. Round barrel vault and tall columns.
>
> *Mauriac.* Octagonal tower like those of Auvergne. Porch with columns resting on lions in Lombard manner.
>
> *Souillac.* Besides sculptures mentioned above is interesting for its domes.
>
> *Lescure, Le Monastier, Saint-Rambert, Saint-Guilhem-le-Desert,* etc.

Chapter III

GOTHIC

Although most people can recognise a Gothic church when they see one, nobody has yet succeeded in finding a satisfactory definition of the term. It was, of course, applied at first as a term of reprobation by those who were so obsessed by the canons of Vitruvius that they failed to appreciate the freedom and romance of a less conventional style, but as modern research traces some of its origins back to the northern and eastern races the name is not wholly inappropriate. It is not merely a question of detail. If we take the pointed as opposed to the round arch as its essential characteristic, our definition fails, as the pointed arch was known in Burgundy and the south before the end of the eleventh century, and round arches are not infrequently met with in purely Gothic churches. The ribbed cross-vault too played an important part in the development of Gothic style, but its problems were almost worked out in the Romanesque period, and many noble Gothic churches, especially in England, were not vaulted at all. We cannot depend on the buttressing system, as flying buttresses were not required if a church was not vaulted, and they were only accepted with reserve outside the Ile-de-France. It was because they thought that by reproducing all these features they could recreate the Gothic style that our forefathers of the Gothic Revival came to grief. For true Gothicness, if we may use such a word, is a spirit rather than a code. It was the natural way of building worked out by generations of men who were working freehand in a material to which they had been brought up, and proceeding step by step by experiment, ready to welcome any new ideas, and finally stretching their material to the utmost in attempting to realise in stone the ambitions of an age whose creative instincts found their chief outlet in building more and yet more magnificent churches. If the pointed arch was almost universally

41

adopted, it was because of its manifest practical advantages; if the flying buttress was used, it was because of its engineering possibilities enabling a stone fire-proof vault to be raised to a great height without blocking the windows; if the nature of sculpture both of the human form and of foliage changes in character, it is only because increasing skill enabled the carvers to give up the Romanesque conventions in the new freedom which taught every man to work out his problems by reference to nature rather than to precedent. If, then, text-book methods compel an analysis of details, we must not let these blind us to the greater issues, lest we fail to see the wood because of the trees. For the power of Gothic resided not in any particular forms but in the whole-hearted adoption of such forms as suited its purpose for the building up of a great system of balancing thrust with counter-thrust, and so making the utmost of available material. The Ile-de-France did not invent the pointed arch or the ribbed vault, but it was there that the full possibilities of this form of construction were most fully realised, and there that the style was first brought to perfection and afterwards accomplished its greatest triumphs.

The last half of the twelfth and first half of the thirteenth centuries witnessed an outburst of building enthusiasm which has never been equalled. The new art of more scientific building in the new style coincided with a change in social conditions. Hitherto the main demand had come from the monasteries, and the great abbeys had outshone in size and magnificence the cathedrals of the bishops, for William the Conqueror's scheme for uniting monastery and cathedral on the old Saxon plan, as at Canterbury or Durham, was not favoured in France. The growth of the royal power which made Paris the centre of a more powerful kingdom, the growth of the towns and the encouragement by the king of the communes as a balance to his more powerful nobles, all tended to the spread of local patriotism. Prosperity was beginning to undermine the strict rule of the monasteries and with their declining austerities there followed a falling-off in popular estime. The bishops were thus in a position to take advantage of the opportunity to stir up popular enthusiasm for each town or commune to strive with its neighbours as to which could build the finest church. Letters still exist describing the wonderful scenes when the whole population turned out to assist in the construction of the great new churches. At Chartres, after the fire, rich and poor alike harnessed themselves to the carts which carried the stone up the hill, and many notable miracles were performed on the occasion. Under such conditions progress was rapid, but projects of such an ambitious nature were undertaken that many of them were never completed, and final touches were left to be added slowly by subsequent generations.

TRANSITIONAL AND EARLY GOTHIC OF THE TWELFTH CENTURY

We saw in the previous chapter how the Romanesque masons were facing the problems which confronted the medieval builders, and how the principles which were to solve them had already been worked out in embryo. It only remained to accept them whole-heartedly and develop them to their fullest capacity.

It has been argued that there was no Transition period in the Ile-de-France, and it can be accepted that the new Gothic style was victorious in Northern France much more quickly than in England. Certain Romanesque features, such as the round arch, were, however, retained for many ornamental features until nearly the end of the twelfth century, even when the pointed arch had been adopted for all constructional purposes.

The fine church at Saint-Germer may be taken as a good example of the Transition. There is no definite record of its date, but there is reason to believe it to have been built *c.* 1120–40. It retains the round arch for all the original windows and for the roomy Romanesque tribunes, but has the plain quadripartite ribbed vault of pure Gothic form, supported on shafts rising from the ground, and there is a kind of embryo flying buttress over the tribunes, though still under the aisle roof. The construction is solid and features heavy, and the rough zig-zag, or chevron, ornament round the arches of the apse still carries on the older tradition, but most of the essentials of the Gothic plan are here adopted, though still in an experimental way (pls. 111, 112).

The nave of the cathedral of Le Mans is also an interesting Transitional work (pl. 113). It is a reconstruction, by Bishop William during the years 1145–58, of the old eleventh-century church, of which the bay next the crossing and the aisles are retained. He introduced the alternate bay system, with two pointed arches resting on a round pillar between the solid piers supporting the vault. This is built on the system in vogue in Anjou, where domical vaults rise high above the transverse arches—a reminiscence of the south-western domes of the preceding period (pls. 40–42), to which reference will be made in describing local schools (see p. 55).

The church in which Gothic style was first fully realised is usually taken to have been the abbey of Saint-Denis, just outside Paris, built under Abbot Suger, who wrote a description of the work. It was begun in 1137 and finished about 1144. Unfortunately the haste with which it was built, and possibly an imperfect realisation of the need for sound buttressing, led to disaster, and the greater part of the church had to be rebuilt little over a hundred years later. Of Suger's building only the west front and the bay between the towers, the crypt and the aisles round the apse (pl. 114) remain, and these have been so much restored that it is unsafe to base too solid a theory on them. If what we see to-day is really Suger's work, it looks as though the new principles of the ribbed cross-vaults had been mastered to such an extent that there must have been earlier experiments in this method of construction which have not come down to us. The round arch was retained for the doorways.

The cathedral of Sens seems to have been contemporary with Saint-Denis, and is better preserved. It is on a grand scale, with a vault

44

about 80 feet high and nearly 50 feet broad. It was begun between 1135 and 1140 and finished, apart from the façade, by 1168. It is built on the alternate bay system, one square double bay of the nave being divided by pointed arches resting on twin pillars (pl. 115) which take the vault of the square bays of the aisles, two of which correspond to each double bay of the central nave. The latter is covered by what is known as a sexpartite vault, in which the cross-ribs from the major piers are reinforced by another pair rising from the intermediate columns (fig. 12). This was a favourite form of vault during the second half of the twelfth century, though the advantages of the

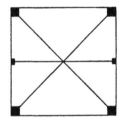
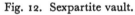
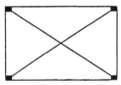

Fig. 12. Sexpartite vault.   Quadripartite vault.

simpler cross-vault (quadripartite), which was more suitable for an oblong bay, led to its abandonment as the style advanced. It was some time before it was realised that the thrust outwards of the ribs in an oblong bay is easier to meet than in a square one where the angle at which the rib meets the buttress is sharper.

The churches of the second half of the twelfth century are particularly attractive, as the work of men experimenting in new methods and working towards new ideals is often more interesting to watch than that in which perfection is attained and forms begin to be stereotyped. Some features of the old Romanesque plan are still retained in work which is otherwise purely Gothic. Thus the roomy triforium galleries, or tribunes, are retained in many churches of this period, as at Noyon (pl. 118) or Laon (pl. 121), and as these were lighted by a window in the back wall there is another small triforium arcade above them to cover the space occupied by the sloping roof over the aisles, making four stories in all, a multiplication of parts which tends to increase the apparent size and dignity of the building. In some cases the round arch continued to be used for the triforium arches (pl. 121) and for windows. In the rounded transepts at Noyon (pl. 119) there are two stories of round-headed arcades or windows and two of pointed, and as the round ones occupy the highest positions the change cannot be caused by a change of design due to lapse of time or slow construction.

The sexpartite vault used at Sens was adopted for most of these churches, and fitted the old Romanesque scheme of the alternate composite pier and round column which was also continued. At Laon the extra shaft supporting the transverse ribs added to those under the cross-ribs makes a bundle of five which alternates with the three in the intermediate sets, and in the western bays these stop at the capitals of the round columns, though attached shafts are used towards the east. At Noyon the alternate bay system is very marked, though its purpose is somewhat obscured by the fact that the original sexpartite vaults collapsed and had to be replaced by the present quadripartite vault, or such parts of it as survived the German bombardments. At Saint-Quiriace, Provins, there is actually an octopartite vault, but the wide spacing was not very happy in effect, and the example was not followed.

During this period the buttressing system was being worked out. In churches with large tribunes their vaults served to abut the thrust of the central vault, but experience proved that this abutment came too low, and the flying buttress was gradually evolved. In many cases these were added later where insufficiently supported vaults were showing signs of weakness. These completed the Gothic scheme of construction which consisted of a framework of stone with each thrust met and held up by a counter-thrust, and a brief account of their development will be given in a later paragraph (see p. 59).

In some of the early Gothic churches decoration was very simple.

Fig. 13. Paris—Notre-Dame (from Viollet-le-Duc).

At Noyon mouldings hardly exist and capitals are plain and coarse, but in other cases the transitional capitals based on the Classical acanthus leaves, but treated with great freedom, are very fine.

The story of twelfth-century Gothic culminates in the famous cathedral of Notre-Dame in Paris. It was begun by Bishop Maurice de Sully in 1163, and the main part of the building, except the west front, was finished by the end of the century. There are roomy

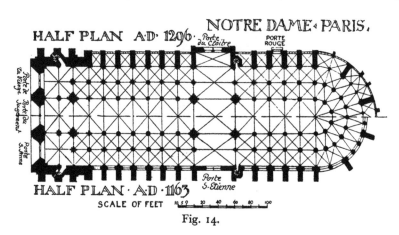

Fig. 14.

tribunes, and though the vault is sexpartite the solid round columns are all alike. If we accept Viollet-le-Duc's opinion, which he backed by restoring two or three bays near the crossing, there were originally round windows above the tribunes, opening into the aisle-roofs above them, as shown in fig. 13. These were suppressed in the middle of the thirteenth century, the aisle-roofs were flattened and the clerestory windows enlarged to give more light. Extra support was given by the huge flying buttresses, which had to be made of vast span to cover the double aisles. The plan (fig. 14) may be taken as typical of that adopted for a great French cathedral. The transepts had no projection originally except in the upper story, but after chapels had been added between the buttresses they were extended one bay.

48

Other examples of Transitional and Early Gothic:

Blois. Saint-Laumer. Choir second half of twelfth century. High vaults ribbed, aisles groined in Romanesque style. Ribbed cupola over crossing. Nave thirteenth century.

Saint-Leu-d'Esserent. Choir *c.* 1180, nave *c.* 1210. Besides western tower there are two more at the springing of the apse.

Poissy. Mid-twelfth century. Much restored and rebuilt.

Mantes. c. 1200, inspired by Paris. Triforium of apse covered by barrel vaults at right angles to axis of nave.

Chalons. Saint-Alpin. Built *c.* 1136, but apparently reconstructed and vaulted towards the end of the twelfth century.

THE THIRTEENTH CENTURY

During the first half of the thirteenth century Gothic art reached its full development. Chartres was rebuilt after the fire of 1194, Reims after that of 1210, Rouen after that of 1200, while Amiens was begun *c.* 1220, Beauvais *c.* 1225, and Bourges, Coutances, the choirs of Le Mans and Auxerre all date from this period.

In all these except Bourges the quadripartite vault replaces the sexpartite, the tribunes are suppressed in order to give greater height to the main arcade and lengthen the clerestory windows, and the system of flying buttresses is fully worked out. The main columns are usually cylindrical with four smaller shafts attached to carry the vaulting shafts and the arcade, and the triforium, unlike the English type, has a back wall behind its narrow passage, instead of opening into the roof-space over the aisles. In many cases the aisles are doubled, especially in the choir. The plans of Amiens and Bourges may be taken as typical (figs. 15, 16), showing a vast hall of overwhelming magnificence when seen from the western doors, and quite different from the long low English cathedral with its projecting transepts and screens, retaining something of the old Romanesque and monastic traditions.

The complete Gothic system of balancing-thrust with counter-thrust, of economising material and building up the cathedral as a

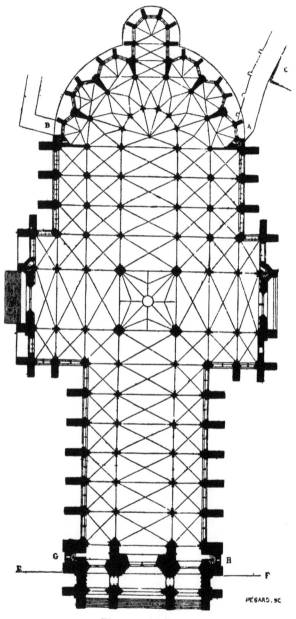

Fig. 15. Amiens.

vast framework of stone, making the containing walls between the buttresses a mere curtain which could be pierced by larger and larger windows till the whole church appears to be mainly walled by the wonderful thirteenth-century glass, is brought to perfection.

These churches are on an enormous scale; though not so long as some English cathedrals they are much wider, and often half as high again. Amiens approaches nearest to the complete Gothic ideal. The vault inside rises to a height of about 140 feet above the pavement, 40 feet higher than that of Westminster Abbey, and the whole construction appears to be very light, supported as it is by enormous flying buttresses. It was begun at the nave, unlike the usual practice, and the choir which appears to have been reached only in the second half of the century has the back walls of the triforium pierced by windows and little gablets over the arches, which add to the richness of effect even if more suitable for the exterior. The whole balance and proportions of the interior, the magnificent thirteenth-century sculpture of the cavernous west porches (pl. 189), and the splendid early sixteenth-century carving of the stalls, all combine to make up the marvellous whole. The only criticism which can be fairly made is that in the exterior view the enormous bulk of the church with its lofty roof serves to dwarf the towers and gives it an outline which cannot compete with that of our smaller English cathedrals with their picturesque medley of gables and towers (pl. 130). This criticism, however, cannot be applied universally to French cathedrals as the groups of towers at Laon and Coutances can bear comparison with anything anywhere.

Chartres and Reims are not quite so lofty, 120–125 feet under the vaults, and are more solidly built. Bourges is a vast hall without any break for a transept. It has double aisles, the inner one having its own triforium and clerestory, giving the effect of a five-storied building. This arrangement is repeated with great success in the choirs of Coutances (pl. 151) and Le Mans (fig. 141), though in these the triforium of the central part has been suppressed, and the lofty columns, doubled round the apse, are very impressive.

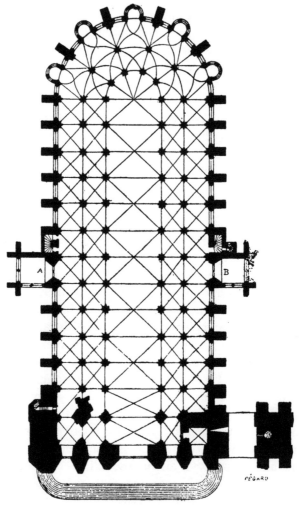

Fig. 16. Bourges.

52

At Beauvais ambition led to disaster. A vault 157 feet high was planned to exceed all other medieval buildings, but it partially collapsed a few years after its erection, and was only completed by adding an extra pier between each of the original ones (see pl. 137). This disaster led to a depletion of the available funds, and the nave was never even begun. In the fifteenth century the huge transepts were added, and neglecting previous warning a tower over 500 feet high was erected over the crossing. This too fell, and it was only possible to patch up the damage, leaving the choir and transept as a most impressive fragment. The vast height is all the more imposing in so short a building, and the triforium is pierced by windows and united in a single composition with the 57-foot-high clerestory windows. Double aisles, the inner with its three stories, as at Bourges, complete what was intended to have been the mightiest church in Christendom (pl. 136).

In one or two cases, as at Rouen, the old four-story plan was continued, but as the work went on it was decided to raise the height of the aisles by abolishing their vaults and leaving the vault of the tribunes above them to serve to cover them. The arcade therefore leading to the tribunes opens into nothing, but a narrow passage is engineered by corbelling out a kind of bracket over the aisle (pl. 143). A similar change took place at Meaux, where again we have a kind of triforium arch opening into the aisle in the choir, while in the nave it has been removed altogether and the main arches raised (pl. 166).

As the century progressed the tendency noted in the choir at Amiens to combine triforium and clerestory into one design was developed till the triforium became little more than a continuation of the upper windows. The buildings became more and more a framework with the curtain walls reduced to the smallest possible extent, and the whole space between the buttresses opened up into great windows in which the glorious thirteenth-century jewelled glass could be placed, the most gorgeous form of decoration ever invented. Such a building as the choir at Troyes (pl. 167) became a lantern of glass in which the visible stone supports are reduced to the minimum, and the whole weight of the vault is held up by comparatively slender shafts reinforced by the scaffolding of flying buttresses outside. Here the effect of the glass, in spite of patching and restoration, is perhaps even more over-whelming in its splendour than the earlier and even finer glass at Chartres or Bourges.

This attenuation of the stonework is carried to an extreme in the church of Saint-Urbain at Troyes, built during the last years of the thirteenth century. In this the fine stone available enabled the builders to treat it almost like metal, and the whole church seems a mere cage of glass (pls. 169, 170).

The choir of the pretty cathedral at Sées in Normandy is a work of c. 1300, and is so lightly built owing to this carrying of economy of material to an extreme, and to insufficient foundations, that very large sums have had to be spent on restoration. It has the triforium merged in the upper windows, and crocketed gables over the main arches, following the scheme initiated at Amiens (pl. 165).

LOCAL SCHOOLS

The Ile-de-France was so prolific and exerted such a wide influence that it tended to swamp local developments, and these were of much less importance in the thirteenth than in the twelfth century. Never-theless, certain tendencies can be noted in special districts, only the most striking of which need be dealt with here.

In the *south-west*, or rather middle-west, Romanesque traditions lingered on, and in adapting the Gothic ribbed vault to churches built on the old plan a special type was developed. The cathedral of Angers is built on the plan of one of the wide aisleless domed churches of the district; it has heavy transverse arches dividing the building into squares and between these the bulky ribs of a cross-vault rise to

54

a point between 9 and 10 feet above the points of the transverse arches, thus producing an effect very like that of a dome although constructed on the ribs in true Gothic fashion. This vault is some 54 or 55 feet wide as compared with about 48 feet in the immensely loftier vault of Amiens, and is thus a very bold experiment for the time when it was built, *c.* 1150 (pl. 171). This *Angevin* type of domed vault assumed a rather different form as time went on. The ribs, which have less strain on them in the domical shaped vault, became much lighter, and extra ribs were run from the top of the wall and transverse arches to the common centre. Several churches in Angers are vaulted on this system, and elsewhere the cathedral at Poitiers (pl. 172) follows the same plan. This is a work of the second half of the twelfth century, and follows another Romanesque tradition, for the aisles are made almost the same height as the central nave, so that their vaults support the central one, and windows in the outer walls can be placed high enough to light the whole space. There is a good example of this type of vault in the thirteenth-century church of Le Puy-Notre-Dame.

Normandy, too, produced a style with marked characteristics though the influence of the Ile-de-France was strongly felt, and the greater churches follow the usual French plan and elevation. They are usually less lofty, the vaults of Rouen and Coutances being about 92 feet high, and there was therefore more room for the development of towers. The outline of Coutances (pl. 150) with its two western spires and central lantern is very different from that of Amiens. Square towers with very tall belfry lights and often crowned with spires are particularly fine in Normandy, and that of Saint-Pierre at Caen may be taken as typical (pl. 193 b). Mouldings are much richer and more numerous than elsewhere in France, bringing these churches much nearer to English models in this respect, and foliage sculpture is more profusely used than figure-work. Small rosettes, sometimes filled with beautiful foliage, are placed in the spandrels over the arches of the main arcade, and give a rich effect. A round abacus over the capitals

55

is common, instead of the square or octagonal form usual in France, and is another feature in which Normandy approaches English practice. The rose window of the façade, which is so prominent a feature in the Ile-de-France, is rare in Normandy.

Champagne shows certain characteristics of its own, but they are hardly sufficient to separate it from the Ile-de-France. *Burgundy* has a rather more distinctive style, in which southern feeling is more felt. The lofty churches of the Ile-de-France are rare, and the old two-story plan of Vézelay was much favoured, merely substituting a ribbed for a groined vault, and pointing the arches. As the churches are usually of moderate dimensions, flying buttresses are also used with moderation, and comparatively small clerestory windows do not occupy the whole space of the curtain wall under the vaults. The larger churches, such as Saint-Benigne (pl. 175) and Notre-Dame at Dijon have the three stories, with a very simple triforium, and a plain apse without ambulatory. This plan also occurs in Champagne, as in the fine church of Saint-Yved de Braisne (pl. 158), and in this province Burgundian and French styles seem to effect one another to some extent. Cistercian influence, which demanded extreme simplicity and absence of ornament, was an important power in Burgundy. The best example of this type is at Pontigny, begun c. 1150. It follows the severe plan adopted in the earlier abbey church at Fontenay (pl. 77) except that the vault of the nave is of the cross-ribbed type, and those of the aisles and transepts groined in the old Romanesque fashion. Later, c. 1180–1200, an eastern extension was carried out to provide more chapels, and a simplified ambulatory plan was adopted with radiating chapels enclosed by a continuous wall and roof (pls. 128, 129). There is a plain wall instead of a triforium, and all details are reduced to austere simplicity.

In the *south* the thirteenth-century was not one of progress or prosperity. The cruel crusade against the Albigenses spread ruin

56

everywhere, and the great building enthusiasm of the north found no place. Here and there great churches were built by imported masons from the north, as at Clermont, Narbonne and Limoges towards the later part of the thirteenth century, though most of them were not finished till later. They seem like foreign intruders among the numerous Romanesque churches which survive, and, like Cologne, seem to miss something of the spontaneous natural growth of Northern France and to be copies rather than the genuine article. It was not until the fourteenth century that a real southern Gothic style was evolved, discussion of which must be postponed to the following chapter.

VAULTING

The different forms of stone vault have already been mentioned. When once the quadripartite vault had been perfected, it was used with little modification almost to the end of the Gothic period, though

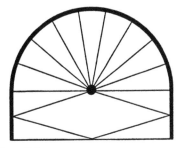

Fig. 17. Vaulting of Apse.

elaborations were sometimes contrived in late Flamboyant work, especially in the smaller vaults of aisles and chapels.

In the apse where a number of ribs converge on a common centre a strong transverse rib was needed to resist the pressure, but this was reduced by adding two ribs of half a bay west of the curved portion, which opposed the thrust from the opposite direction, as shown in the accompanying diagram (fig. 17). When we come to a great church

57

with double aisles forming an ambulatory round the apse, and bordered with a ring of chapels, there was room for great ingenuity in adjusting the ribs to the necessary curves. For these more complicated problems the reader must be referred to more elaborate treatises than the present brief introduction.

An interesting point is the difference of method in dealing with the web of the vault between the ribs in England and France. In France each "voutain" or vaulting stone was carefully shaped for its position so as to bring the joints to an even line in forming an arch over a triangular space. In England less scientific and more rough-and-ready methods were adopted (fig. 18); stones of the same shape were employed, with the result that when they met at the crown of the arch there was a saw-edge, which was neither so strong nor sightly as the straight French joint. Extra ribs, therefore, were introduced to cover the joint and at the same time reduce the width of the space to be covered. This enabled them to flatten the curves and to keep the ridge of the vault level. A ridge-rib then bound the whole design firmly together, extra small ribs called liernes were added to strengthen the framework, which at the same time afforded opportunities for forming pretty star patterns, and carved bosses were placed to cover the intersection of the ribs.

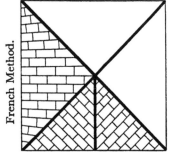

Fig. 18. English Method.

In this way an apparent carelessness and lack of scientific imagination led in actual practice to the production of finer and more beautiful vaults than are to be found in the great French cathedrals, whose great height would have rendered elaborate carving ineffective when seen from the ground.

58

The buttress system, which enabled a stone vault to be supported at a great height from the ground, is one of the essential features of the complete Gothic church. It has been suggested that the problem was solved by cutting up the lateral walls of the church into sections and placing each section at right angles to its original position. The roof could then be placed on the top and the spaces between them were available for a mere curtain wall, which had little work to do and could be pierced by large windows. A general idea of the balance of forces in a Gothic cathedral can be obtained better from the accompanying diagram from Viollet-le-Duc (fig. 19) than from any lengthy description.

The necessary abutment for the vault in Romanesque churches was supplied by the aisle-vaults, or in larger buildings by the vaults of the tribunes and aisles. At Saint-Germer the vaults of the tribunes are reinforced at intervals by rudimentary flying buttresses, which are still kept below the outer roof. As, however, the churches grew loftier and tribunes went out of fashion, the buttresses had to be brought above the roofs if the thrust had to be met at the proper place. The earliest flying buttresses were very plain, simple ramping arches leading to a solid wall or tower of masonry, as at Saint-Rémi at Reims (pl. 122). Later it was found that they were more effective if they were given two arches, one above the other, and weight was added to the supporting piers by adding little edicules or pinnacles. These gave the Gothic masons an opportunity of using a constructive necessity to provide an ornamental feature. The extraordinarily solid buttresses of Chartres were provided with niches for statues (pl. 176a), and the finest solution of the problem is to be found at Reims, where tall pinnacles containing large angel-statues with outspread wings are used to weight the buttress piers and so turn the outward thrust into a downward direction where it can be easily met (pl. 178b).

59

Fig. 19. Amiens.

Where there was a double aisle the buttress arches had to be of very wide span, as at Notre-Dame de Paris, where they had to be largely reconstructed by Viollet-le-Duc, or at Coutances (pl. 150), but the more usual method was to provide a double flight of arches with a pier midway resting on the pillars dividing the aisles. When both uprights are crowned with pinnacles, as at Le Mans (pl. 140), a veritable forest of buttresses and spirelets is produced.

The arches of the flying buttresses were usually provided with channels to conduct the rain-water from the roof gutters to projecting gargoyles beyond the outer walls. In some cases, as at Amiens (pl. 131), as the arch had to be applied too low to collect this water, a straight channel was built above it supported on a light open arcade, of very decorative effect.

WINDOWS

In the Transitional period round-headed windows are frequently retained, and even when they are given up windows of very much the same shape, except that they are pointed, are used. It has been the custom to divide windows into two styles, the *Lancet* and the *Geometric* (or "Rayonnant" as the French call it). The first lancets were wider than those to which we are accustomed in England (except under French influence at Canterbury), though long tall lancets occasionally occur in particular positions especially in Normandy, as at Coutances (pl. 153), or on towers. As more light was required it became customary to group lancets in pairs, as at Noyon (pl. 119), and sometimes in threes, especially in Champagne, as at Saint-Rémi at Reims (pl. 122) or Chalons (pl. 123). The next development was to place a circular window above them, as at Chartres (pl. 178a), where the circles have become small rose windows. When these lancets and circles were enclosed by a containing arch we have what has been called "plate-tracery". In such windows the view from inside is chiefly considered, but when attention was also paid to the outside the spandrels were pierced, from which the step to "bar-tracery" was a short one. At first circles only were placed over the lights, and star-shaped openings were produced by cusps, as in the tower windows of the transept at Reims (pl. 178b), or in the cathedral at Chalons-sur-Marne (pl. 163). Later trefoils, as in the apse chapels at Amiens (pl. 131), quatrefoils or other geometric forms were used, but window tracery tended to become rather stereotyped and the Geometric forms continued in use until the coming of the Flamboyant style, without any of the rich variety of English "Decorated". Mullions were often very thin and stability depended to some extent on the iron bars supporting the magnificent painted glass. In large windows an even number of lights was preferred, the English fashion of an uneven number with a central panel being more suited to a square east end than to the curved French chevet.

The increasing size of windows was, no doubt, influenced by the development of the coloured glass which formed the most gorgeous decoration for a building ever devised. It took the form of a mosaic of pieces of brilliant glass in which dark blue and rich ruby predominated, fixed together by leading, with details put in in black with a firm touch. The result is not a naturalistic picture but a pattern made up of glowing jewels. In the lower windows of the aisles little scenes from the Bible, the lives of the saints, or theological types, are grouped into roundels or other geometric forms enclosed in solid iron bars, while the upper clerestory windows usually are filled with single figures of prophets or saints.

Rose, or wheel, windows are favoured for the façade or transept front. The finest of these is that of the west front of Chartres, said to be some 46 feet across (pl. 179a). It dates from the beginning of the thirteenth century when plate tracery was still the vogue. In later examples bar tracery replaces the circles, and in the second half of the century the spaces between the wheel and the containing arch were pierced and traceries added to throw the whole glazed end of the building into one composition, including the triforium gallery below, as at Chalons (pl. 179b).

Façade and Porch

The west front was usually the last part of a great church to be undertaken, though preparations for providing the sculpture may have been made from the beginning. The result was that the original design was frequently left incomplete, and the upper parts added in a later style. The composition therefore varies considerably, but that of Notre-Dame de Paris may be taken as typical of the normal design (pl. 181). Even this took some time to build: it seems to have been begun in 1208 and the tops of the towers were not reached till nearly the middle of the century. Some sculpture, too, prepared c. 1163, was adapted for use in one of the doorways. The main entrance to most great churches was at the west, and consisted of three great cavernous portals, filled with sculptures, and leading into the three main divisions of the nave of the church. Above these was the gallery of kings, with statues probably representing the royal line of Judah, ancestors of our Lord. Above these again was the great rose, and then an open-work gallery connecting the bases of the towers, and masking the gable. In a number of cases only one of the two towers was ever completed, and that, too, in a later style, while in others, as at Sens, one tower collapsed and necessitated the reconstruction of a great part of the front. Detailed description of the most important examples is unnecessary if reference is made to the illustrations at the end of this book.

The porches usually have a double door divided by a central pillar, or "trumeau", which supports the lintel, above which the flat space up to the enclosing arch, called the "tympanum", is filled with sculpture in high relief divided up into a series of bands. The most popular subjects are the Last Judgment, the Coronation of the Virgin, the Madonna and Child and Nativity scenes, or illustrations of the lives of local saints. The sides of the porch are lined with large statues (pl. 192), at first placed against pillars and of long thin proportions, afterwards of natural shape and gradually freed from their architectural tie to the shafts till they were placed in a row of niches. The mouldings round the arches are filled with smaller figures and groups, often of great interest and beauty and throwing much light on medieval theology and thought.

At Bourges, where there are double aisles to the nave, there are five great double porches, standing above a fine flight of steps, producing a most imposing effect (pl. 190).

In some of the greatest cathedrals the transept fronts were treated as additional façades, provided with low towers and porches. Those at Chartres (pls. 186, 187) even surpass the older western front in magnificence. Apart from these transept doorways, side porches like those at Wells, Canterbury or Lincoln, are rare, but a fine example exists at Notre-Dame, Chalons-sur-Marne.

TOWERS AND SPIRES

The normal plan of a thirteenth-century cathedral has two towers at the west end, and in Normandy a central lantern tower, with the lower stage open to the church, is favoured. That at Coutances is particularly fine both inside (pl. 195a) and out (pl. 150). In the great Ile-de-France cathedrals, like Amiens, the scale is so great that a central tower would have been dangerous and a light flèche is substituted. The attempt to build such a tower at Beauvais ended in disaster. Extra towers were sometimes built on each side of the transept fronts, as at Chartres (pl. 187) and Rouen, but were seldom carried up to their full height. At Chartres there are two more small towers, making eight in all, at the springing of the curve of the apse. Laon comes nearest to the ideal, as five of its seven towers are carried up to their full height, though they lack the spires for which they must have been designed.

The general design of the towers can best be seen by reference to the illustrations. The square plan is the commonest, especially in

Normandy, but the outline is sometimes complicated by stair-turrets at the corners, as at Coutances (pl. 183). Where a spire was built or intended, an octagonal course is often inserted between the square tower and the spire, and the transition is masked by lofty pinnacles, producing a pyramidal design. This form was mostly favoured in the Ile-de-France, and the most graceful example is the spire at Senlis (pl. 193a). In Normandy, as in England, the division between tower and spire is more emphasised and the octagonal stage omitted.

Certain local types of tower are to be found in the southern districts. At Toulouse a special design was worked out for building in brick, the material available there (pl. 196a), and at Limoges octagonal towers with corner buttresses are so arranged that the angles come in the middle of the face (pl. 196c). Fortified churches, which look more like castles with machicolated cornices and no windows, are also to be found in this disturbed area (pl. 196b).

SCULPTURE

The sculptured decoration formed such an important part of a medieval church that even an outline description would require a volume to itself, and the reader must be referred to special works on the subject. The foliage carving of the Transitional period is largely based on the Corinthian types of the preceding age, but treated with ever-increasing freedom. The capitals of the western bays at Saint-Rémi at Reims are fine examples (pl. 198a) with their double row of out-curving serrated leaves. The curious whorls at Chalons-sur-Marne (pl. 198b) seem an elaboration of much earlier interlacing designs, while the capital at Laon, shown in pl. 198c, seems a combination of the two. The fine scroll-work at Rouen (pl. 197), Paris and Mantes carry on the Romanesque traditions of Bourges (pl. 75) or Burgundy.

In Normandy a simplified conventional type of foliage lasted longer than elsewhere, though it never adopted the "stiff-leaf" form so popular in England. The nearest approach is shown in such beautiful little friezes or cornices as may be found in the lantern at Coutances (pl. 195a). Leaves based on natural forms, but not slavishly copied, and slightly conventionalised are seen in such masterly scroll-work as fills a small door-head at Bayeux (pl. 199a).

Elsewhere during the thirteenth century men turned more and more to direct observation of nature. In the north porch at Chartres are careful studies of plant forms (pl. 199b), and the capitals at Reims and Auxerre are covered with beautiful renderings of leaves, sometimes mixed with little figures (pl. 200).

Other examples. Thirteenth century:

> *Tours Cathedral.* Begun 1268 with the choir. Transept and eastern bays of nave fourteenth century. Façade not finished till 1547 in Flamboyant style, with dome-like caps to towers showing Renaissance feeling.
>
> *Lyons Cathedral.* Romanesque apse without aisles, *c.* 1160, vaulted *c.* 1190. Choir, transept and crossing 1192–1245. Nave late thirteenth century. Façade, lower part early fourteenth, but upper part not completed till 1480. Has four short towers, two at west end and two over transepts.
>
> *Fécamp Abbey.* Reconstruction begun after fire in 1170, but work seems to have been going on till 1297.
>
> *Norrey.* Fine tower. Rich foliage of third quarter of thirteenth century.
>
> *Paris. Sainte-Chapelle.* Built by St Louis to hold the Crown of Thorns. Consecrated 1248. Double church over a large crypt. No pillars—rich glass, but much over-restored.
>
> *Dijon. Notre-Dame.* Good example of Burgundian Gothic of thirteenth century.
>
> *Fine towers or spires* at Vernouillet, Caen Saint-Sauveur, Saint-Père-sous-Vézelay, Bernières, Chateau-Landon.
>
> *Open western porch* (or narthex) at Saint-Père-sous-Vézelay and Semur-en-Auxois (a Burgundian feature).

THE FOURTEENTH CENTURY

This in France was not a period of rapid progress. Disastrous wars ravaged the land and in the middle of the century the Black Death brought everything to a standstill. In the last quarter some revival took place and some encouragement of the arts was given by the courts of Paris and Burgundy, but conditions were very different from those which had produced the early Gothic.

By the fourteenth century the enthusiasm which had inspired the building of the great cathedrals had begun to wane, and it was only with difficulty that funds were raised to complete the ambitious plans made by the earlier generation. New enterprises were comparatively rare, and usually consisted in little more than additions to older buildings. A common development was the addition of chapels between the great projecting buttresses, many of them intended to serve as special meeting places of guilds or memorial chapels for great families. Thus a ring of chapels was added to the choir at Paris, c. 1300, and a little later others of a more advanced style were built between the buttresses at Amiens, Bayeux, and elsewhere.

The nave at Auxerre is a good example of fourteenth-century style. It was begun after 1334, but the vault was not finally completed till the fifteenth century. It is a logical but somewhat cold design; vaulting shafts rise from the floor without any break, mouldings are shallow and capitals reduced to insignificance. There is a triforium to correspond with the earlier choir, and enormous geometric windows fill the whole space between vault and buttresses and afford a fine field for gorgeous coloured glass (pl. 203).

Generally speaking the complete Gothic scheme evolved in the thirteenth century is carried on with little fresh inspiration, and an increasing tendency to produce a stereotyped and efficient if uninspired building. After such churches as Saint-Urbain at Troyes, or the choir of the cathedral in the same town, there was not much room for further progress on the same lines. The nave of Troyes bears some resemblance to that of Auxerre, but the triforium is glazed and the mouldings richer. With its double aisles and chapels it presents a magnificent forest of columns and arches, and the sense of breadth and spaciousness is increased by the more moderate height of the vault. It seems to have been begun in the fourteenth century to which the lower part belongs, but construction proceeded very slowly, and the vault was not finished till the end of the fifteenth century (pl. 202).

In this period windows were usually large, filling the whole space available, and tracery tends to become slight with very light stonework. The form of it remains that of the Geometrical period with little or none of the variety developed in the Decorated style contemporary in England. Foliage is naturalistic, but tends to become confused in outline, and capitals lose the feeling for architectural form in a mass of leaves stuck on to the bell without much formal arrangement. Glass introduces more variety of colour and there are more light colours and taller canopies, but something of the jewel-like splendour of the earlier mosaic glass is lost.

Sculpture becomes more the job of specialists, and its gradual divorce from its architectural surroundings deprives it of some of its nobler qualities. It seems conceived on a smaller scale, and though c. 1300 it is often exquisite in the delicacy and charm of its detail, as in the porches of Auxerre or the reliefs of the apse-chapels at Paris, it seldom reaches the noble statuesque quality of the best thirteenth-century work. Statues are no longer column-figures, and are ranged in separate niches, as in the porches at Bordeaux or Rampillon (pl. 205).

Perhaps the most original buildings of this period are to be found in the south, where northern thirteenth-century Gothic had never felt quite at home. In the Romanesque period the domed churches had accustomed men to wide aisleless naves, and under the newer conditions a somewhat similar plan was evolved with extremely wide vaults and no pillars to interrupt the scheme of a single vast hall. The frequent use of brick and the need for producing a building which could be used as a fortress in time of need may also have led to this design. In it flying buttresses exposed to the weather could be avoided as there were no aisles, and the substantial buttresses required to support the vast vaults were brought inside, under the roof, and the space between them used as chapels.

68

The most remarkable churches of this type are the great fortress cathedral at Albi, the cathedral at Perpignan, and the churches of Saint-Vincent at Carcassonne and Saint-Bertrand-de-Comminges.

Outside, Albi Cathedral presents the appearance of a great red-brick castle with walls some 130 feet high, absolutely plain with the ends of the buttresses covered by rounded bastions and tall narrow slits of windows high above the ground (pl. 206). Inside, the vault has a span of 62 feet, and the great buttresses enclose two ranges of chapels one above the other. The plan is sound and workman-like, and the general effect on this scale is impressive. The absence of the grace and beauty of northern arcades is compensated for by the astonishingly rich late screen which encloses the choir, and by the preservation of the original sixteenth-century wall paintings (pl. 207).

The cathedral at Perpignan is on a very similar plan, but the chapels between the buttresses are only in one story. The vault, 53 feet wide, has the ribs of the ordinary Gothic type, but the web between them is constructed on the old Roman plan of a concrete filling containing pottery jars to lighten the weight (pl. 208).

Saint-Vincent at Carcassonne has a vault of 66 feet span, only surpassed by that of the Spanish cathedral of Gerona.

It is difficult to select many typical examples of fourteenth-century style, as most of the thirteenth-century churches left unfinished were completed by very slow stages and work went on spasmodically until the fifteenth century. Thus the great church at Saint-Quentin was begun in the middle of the thirteenth century; its double transepts seem to be of fourteenth-century date and the nave fifteenth, while the façade was never finished. The choir of Saint-Ouen at Rouen is one of the most complete examples, but the nave and central tower had to wait for the fifteenth century and the west front for the nineteenth.

Other examples. Fourteenth century:

Carcassonne. Saint-Nazaire Choir. Elegant addition to eleventh-century nave, with light pillars and large windows. Completed 1321.

La Chaise Dieu (1342–70). Belongs rather to southern types. Low and wide nave with narrow aisles of same height.

Chartres. Saint-Pierre. Apse said to have been finished *c.* 1310; nave earlier.

Saint-Satur. Begun 1361 and left unfinished 1405. Choir and transepts good example of late fourteenth-century work.

Bordeaux. Choir and transept.

Rodez (1272–*c.* 1500).

Bayonne. Begun in thirteenth century, but mostly dates from fourteenth.

Clermont-Ferrand. (Unfinished when consecrated 1346.)

Chapter IV

FLAMBOYANT

During the fifteenth century a new style of architecture came into fashion and completely transformed the appearance of the newer churches. Its first beginnings can be noted in the last quarter of the fourteenth century, as in some of the side-chapels at Amiens *c.* 1375; its greatest output was in the second half of the fifteenth and first quarter of the sixteenth centuries, and it lasted till ousted by the Italian Renaissance ideas which came in with Queen Catherine de Medicis.

It brought little change in the plan or even the elevation of the Gothic church, but the whole method of decoration was revolutionised. As has been well said "decorated architecture replaced architectural decoration".

In window tracery the old Geometric or "Rayonnant" forms had continued throughout the greater part of the fourteenth century with little change and none of the variety and invention shown by the Decorated style in England, but suddenly a new type was evolved in which the double reversed curve, or "ogee", became the basic feature, and the openings assumed the flame-like shapes which have given the name of "Flamboyant" to the style. In some ways this was a natural development, as the placing of a circle on a couple of pointed arches leaves an awkward corner where the tip of the arches curves away from the circle, a defect which the reversed curve does away with, while the narrow flame-shaped openings can be adapted more easily to fit into the containing arch. Two shapes, especially, form the basis of many windows, and are called by the French "mouchettes" (snuffers) and "soufflets" (bellows), and the accompanying rough diagram will serve to identify them (fig. 20). They can be well seen in the windows from Saint-Ouen at Rouen in pl. 240b.

In the interiors there was a tendency to suppress the triforium, though it is sometimes retained in order to conform to the design of earlier parts of the church, as in the fifteenth-century nave of Saint-Ouen at Rouen, where the choir was of fourteenth-century design. Sometimes, especially in Normandy, an elaborately carved balustrade is carried along the base of the clerestory windows to provide a narrow passage for cleaning or repairs, as in Saint-Jean at Caen (pls. 210, 219b). Mouldings are richer and more carefully studied, with wide

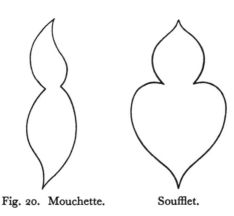

Fig. 20. Mouchette.   Soufflet.

hollows, sometimes of an ogee section, separated by sharply cut ridges or fillets, and are often described as prismatic in shape. The arch mouldings are often carried down to the ground without any interruption by capitals, and thus profoundly alter the shape of the piers and replace the rather feeble bundles of shafts of the fourteenth century. Such capitals as are retained are small or are reduced to narrow bands of foliage with no architectural function. Where there are round pillars, as at Caudebec (pl. 214), the mouldings die into the pillar well above the capital, and from this it is not a far cry to the complete abolition of the capital as at Saint-Maclou, Rouen (pl. 212), Brou (pl. 213), Saint-Pierre, Coutances (pl. 216b), or Sainte-Savine, Troyes (pl. 219a).

Bases rise much higher from the ground and become much more complicated, with sharp-cut fillets and a special treatment for each moulding. A reference to that shown in the illustration from Brou (pl. 213) will show the type better than a long description.

Vaulting on the old quadripartite system is often retained with only slight modifications in the profile of the ribs, but sometimes, especially towards the end of the period, extra ribs were introduced, called "liernes", and these were even multiplied and arranged to form star patterns, as in the aisle at Saint-Riquier (pl. 216a). In small vaults, as at Rue (pl. 241b), extreme elaboration was introduced with pendant bosses and richly carved ribs. Pendant bosses are also found at Saint-Pierre, Caen (pl. 217), and may be due to English suggestions, though the later French vaults seldom reach the standard set by such glorious creations as those of Exeter or Tewkesbury, and never adopted the fan-tracery vault of our Perpendicular style.

Churches of this period seldom reach the dimensions of the great thirteenth-century cathedrals, except when completing those left unfinished, and builders seem to have been satisfied with a more moderate height. The elimination of capitals and other details no longer required for a logical scheme of construction would, in spite of the scientific elaboration of mouldings, have produced a rather severe type of interior had it not been for the extreme richness of the furniture and fittings. Wood-carvers were called in to supply richly sculptured stalls, of which those at Brou and the superb examples at Amiens may be picked out for special mention; marvellously intricate screens were erected to shut off the choir, of which that at Albi has already been mentioned (pl. 207), and that in the church of La Madeleine at Troyes is another fine example (pl. 242). The mason who contrived the latter with its absence of central support was buried beneath it with an inscription on his tomb slab to the effect that he slept safely beneath it without any fear of it falling on him. These "jubés", as they were called, were especially popular in the north-east, and in Flanders over the border.

Foliage, like everything else, underwent a complete transformation. The varied naturalistic leaves of the preceding period were replaced by sharply cut types based on the thistle rather than the vine, or if the latter were used the leaves were made as spikey as possible. The leaves are deeply undercut, and stand out sharply against a background of shadow, and brilliance of effect is sought rather than beauty of form. Good examples may be found at Rue (pl. 243), Caen (pl. 219b), and at Brou (pl. 244b); in the latter Flemish influence is strong and there is just a suggestion of the Classical revival which was beginning to be felt in the early years of the sixteenth century.

It is when we come to the exterior that we find the chief triumphs of Flamboyant architecture. The fifteenth-century builders let themselves go when they planned a façade, a porch or a tower, and produced buildings of astonishing intricacy and fancy. To the purist these may seem overloaded with ornament and restless in conception, but there is a picturesque appeal, and poetic feeling in their lavish recklessness of expenditure in labour and imagination which cannot fail to impress the beholder. The absence of plain surfaces on which to rest the eye is less felt when there is a bold design of structural form behind the overwhelming richness of detail. A more serious criticism is that this intricate lacework of stone exposes too great a surface to the attacks of wind and rain, and some of the finest of these creations have required so much restoration and renewal of detail that they have lost much of their original charm by the substitution of modern mechanical reproductions.

The west front of La Trinité at Vendôme (pl. 220) may be taken as a typical example. The flame-like tracery occupies tympanum and window and even some of the wall-space above, while a lofty open-work gable rises above the main porch. Elaborate cusping runs round the arches and even along those of the flying buttresses, and panelling and niche-work cover the upright supports. The ogee arch is a

74

prominent feature everywhere, and the tracery has none of the restraint of our English Decorated work.

The façades of Auxerre and Troyes (pls. 221, 222), with their bold buttresses and rows of niches—now alas! empty—are very effective compositions, although only one of the two solid towers contemplated has in each case been completed, but perhaps the best idea of the style can be obtained from that of Saint-Riquier, where more of the sculpture survives, and the great porch with its niches and gable occupies the whole centre of the front (pl. 223).

A wonderful new screen of open-work niches and tracery was applied to the old thirteenth-century front of Rouen Cathedral during the first quarter of the sixteenth century, leaving the side doorways of the old front still exposed. This delicate work has required much renewal, and some even of the new statues placed in this exposed position have already begun to show signs of decay, partly perhaps because modern taste does not sanction the medieval method of protecting stone sculpture by the application of paint, which trans- formed the whole front into a gorgeous screen of glowing colours (pl. 224). Rouen also possesses the striking canted front of Saint- Maclou, which has a remarkable array of lofty gables filled with open-work tracery, backed by balustrades, while buttresses and pinnacles alike are covered with a lace-work of stone (pl. 225).

The most satisfactory design for a façade of this period is perhaps that of the unfinished church at Abbeville (pl. 227). Both towers have been completed, and though restoration has robbed many of the details of the fascination felt by those who saw them in their picturesque decay the general effect is a most delightful combination of bold composition combined with richness of detail.

Transept fronts are sometimes almost as splendid as the main façade, though it was no longer customary to flank them with low towers like those of the thirteenth century at Chartres or Rouen. Those of Beauvais, Sens (pl. 228), Evreux (pl. 229) and Senlis (pl. 230) may be specially mentioned.

75

The old triple-porch scheme is often retained, as at Caudebec (pl. 231), but statues were placed in niches with elaborate canopies, and the little scenes in the mouldings are often overcrowded with small figures, so that the delicacy of the work causes them to be ineffective from a distance, especially when it has also led to confusion caused by decay.

The extent to which elaboration of detail could be carried may be seen in the porches at Louviers (pl. 232) and in the magnificent side-portal added to the severe cathedral at Albi by Bishop Louis d'Amboise, which has something of the form of a glorified baldachino (pl. 233).

Towers of this period are often lofty and very picturesque in outline. Fine specimens may be found in the Tour de Beurre at Rouen, at Saint-Omer in the north (pl. 235a), at Clamecy in the centre (pl. 235b) and at Rodez in the south (pl. 234b). The central tower of Saint-Ouen at Rouen is surmounted by a truncated octagon of most effective design (pl. 236). Spires are also of great variety of design and great elaboration. Rising from coronals of pinnacles, enriched with crockets and pierced with decorative openings, or sometimes consisting of a mere framework of stone, they produce a gorgeous effect. The open-work spire at Caudebec (to a great extent rebuilt), the splendid north steeple of Chartres, placed on the old twelfth-century tower (pl. 180), the twin spires rising over the late thirteenth-century façade of the ruined abbey of Saint-Jean-des-Vignes at Soissons (pl. 238), now reduced to worse ruin by German shells, and the wonderful twin spires of Notre-Dame-de-l'Épine, near Chalons-sur-Marne (pl. 237), which give this church such a wonderful outline, may be picked out for special mention.

Finally, when the fashion for things Italian was being introduced in the sixteenth century, we have some very curious experiments in which attempts were made to mix Renaissance detail with the old Gothic plan. The strange attempts to design a Classical form of tracery for the east windows of Saint-Martin at Troyes (pl. 244a) are interesting rather than beautiful, and the same may be said of the extremely rich eastern chapels of Saint-Pierre at Caen (pl. 245), which are perhaps the most ambitious experiment in this direction.

The Origins of the Flamboyant Style

The change from the stereotyped forms of fourteenth-century Gothic to the Flamboyant of the fifteenth is so abrupt and Transitional examples so few that some French authorities have looked for some outside influence to have started it. Thus M. Enlart, starting from the idea that its most characteristic features were the ogee arch, the flowing curvilinear tracery and the complicated lierne vault, found all these fully developed in English Decorated work three-quarters of a century before they became at all common in France. He pointed out that the most numerous examples of the style, and some of the earliest, occur in just those provinces which were in English occupation after the wars of Henry V, and concludes that the style arose from the adoption of ideas developed on this side of the Channel. It must, however, be acknowledged that the result of this adoption of ideas produced something entirely different from the English Decorated, and it would be strange to find a nation so full of imagination and initiative as the French copying a style which had already run its course in England and was becoming obsolete and being replaced by the Perpendicular. In some respects there is a resemblance between the English Perpendicular and French Flamboyant in the use of prismatic mouldings, stilted bases and the rejection of capitals, but there is a world of difference between the stately and business-like Perpendicular and the poetic riot of imagination and fiery picturesqueness of the Flamboyant.

It can, therefore, hardly be claimed that England repaid the debt she owed to France for the introduction of Norman architecture in the eleventh century by the return gift of the style prevalent in France in the fifteenth. So far as English influence can have been felt it

77

cannot have amounted to much more than those suggestions which must naturally have come from intercourse between neighbouring nations brought into contact both in peace and war.

Other examples of Flamboyant not illustrated or mentioned in the text:

Pont de l'Arche. Saint-Vigor. Lace-work architecture partly renewed.
Dijon Chartreuse. 1383–88.
Mézières. Begun 1499.
Saint-Nicholas du Port. 1494–1530. Tall round columns with disappearing mouldings. Lierne vaults and striking façade.
Moulins. Choir (1468–1505). Modern nave.
Quimper. Begun thirteenth century, choir fourteenth, nave and west towers fifteenth.
Auch. Begun 1489, but took two centuries to complete with unfortunate results.
Nantes. Fine fifteenth-century façade. Large cathedral of rather mixed styles, mostly late.
Saint-Lô. 1297–1497. Later style prevails. Two western steeples.
Mont Saint-Michel. Choir (1450–54).
Tréguier. Begun 1339, but only finished in fifteenth-century style.
Façades. Vienne Saint-Maurice; Alençon; Tours; Toul.
Towers. Verneuil; Saint-Pol-de-Léon; Kreisker (spire with remarkable pinnacles, fifteenth century); Bordeaux.

Chapter V

ARCHITECTS AND MASONS

The use of the title "architect" is perhaps a little misleading, as the functions of the medieval designer and the conditions under which he worked were entirely different from those of his modern counterpart. The position has been well summarised by Lethaby in the chapter on French Masons in his *Medieval Art*, and treated at greater length by Henri Stein in *Les Architectes des Cathédrales Gothiques*. Research in the records and especially in the building accounts has unearthed the names of a very large number of master-masons working on various buildings and M. Bauchal has published a dictionary of them. It would obviously be useless to give a list of names here, but a few words as to their position and the conditions under which they worked would not be out of place, as we all feel a natural desire to pay tribute to the men who raised such superb works of art as the great cathedrals.

When scholars first began to enquire into this subject they had an idea that these magnificent churches were designed by monks. This was suggested by the way in which monkish historians attribute the work to the bishop or abbot who commanded it, and who had provided the funds. Even more recently too much has been attributed to a great building-abbot like Suger because he wrote an account of his rebuilding of Saint-Denis. He has even been credited with a great part in the introduction of the full Gothic scheme and ribbed vault, but though he may have drawn up a list of his requirements or even dictated the subjects to be illustrated by carvers or glass-painters, such a man could not have been the architect any more than Henry III was the architect of Westminster Abbey.

When distinguished prelates like William of Volpiano or Lanfranc

79

are credited with introducing the new architecture into Normandy from Lombardy, it could only have been that they were presumed to have had Lombard masons in their train, though, as a matter of fact, the Lombard features in Norman architecture are not very evident, and the part played by the abbots was really little more than the stimulus they gave towards building churches on a much more ambitious scale than had been the fashion hitherto. Except perhaps in the primitive conditions in the Dark Ages when monks went out to found new monasteries in desert places, the monkish architect is really a fiction, and as soon as the monasteries were rich enough to house themselves in a more ambitious way lay masons were called in to do the work. It is, of course, possible that occasionally a mason was admitted as a brother and might become sacrist in charge of the works, but when monks are described as skilful craftsmen it is mentioned usually as an exception, and even these were mostly employed on smaller works of sculpture such as shrines or altar furniture. The plan of St Hugh's great church at Cluny was attributed to St Peter himself, who appeared in a dream to a sick monk named Gunzo, and traced out the plan with cords, but no doubt practical men were called in to supply the details.

In the ordinary way the functions of the modern architect seem to have been divided up. First, we have the patron, king, bishop, abbot, or whoever was the founder and provider of the funds; he may have had rather more say in the matter than would be the case nowadays, and he may have gone over the ground with his assistants stating in a general way what he wanted. Secondly, there was often a master-of-the-works, who was usually a cleric; it was his duty to look after the business side of the building, the payment of the builders and provision of materials. We should now call him clerk of the works. Finally, there were the master-mason and master-carpenter, who were really the men responsible for the design and carrying-out of the details. Of these the master-mason had the most important functions, and should be regarded as the nearest approach to an architect which the

Middle Ages knew. He was not a gentleman artist trained in a drawing office, who provided elaborate working drawings to be mechanically reproduced by the workmen, but was himself trained as a working mason, and was only selected for his greater ability and experience than his fellows. He seems to have produced rough sketches or models for approval, but if we may judge from the famous sketch-book of Villard de Honnecourt, the thirteenth-century master-mason, and from the scanty designs which have come down to us, these must have been very simple, and the work must have needed his constant supervision working along with the other masons employed on the building. We must picture him marking out the plan on the ground, and fixing the exact details and profiles of shaft and moulding —probably on boards—but leaving a certain amount of discretion to the actual carvers in the sculpture and ornament. Each shaped stone seems to have had its mason's mark on it, so that good work could be passed, bad rejected and the responsibility fixed.

The first thing to be done was to erect the masons' lodge, usually a large wooden shed, in which the finer work and sculpture could be prepared, as it seems certain that the bulk of the carving was done before erection. A number of skilled masons worked under the master, and they were of various grades, such as free-masons or hewers, rough-masons and layers, and these specialised groups seem to have increased in the later part of the period under discussion. Imagers, painters and finishers become more and more divided from the building masons as time goes on, and the result of such separation is evident in the changing quality of their productions.

The skilled masons had their servants and a number of labourers attached to them to do the heavy work such as digging, transport and carrying of the stone. It seems likely that the training and early experience of the masons began and was centred in the quarries, where much of the preliminary shaping of the stones was done. In England, at any rate, the masses of carved fragments at Corfe which can still be found show that the Purbeck-marblers prepared shafts and even capitals and more elaborate work on the spot for export. As carriage over medieval roads was a difficult matter, this method would have lightened the loads to be carried, a matter of great importance where water transport was not available.

It was under such conditions that medieval art rose to its perfection. Although the organisation and supervision must have been in the hands of the master, sufficient latitude was allowed to those working under him to put something of their own into their work, and this, combined with slight irregularities in construction, gives a life and vigour to their handicraft which we miss so completely in the mechanically perfect but lifeless work produced when we try to copy or restore the medieval detail under modern machine-minded conditions.

As for the social status of the masons, and especially the master-masons, modern research has produced a certain amount of evidence. The building trade was the most important industry of the time, and its leaders were valued members of the community. It was organised somewhat on the lines still followed in a university where the master of arts or grammar corresponded to the master of masonry, though the stricter rules of the later masonic guilds do not seem to have been fully developed till quite the end of the medieval period.

The sketch-book of Villard de Honnecourt shows that a thirteenth-century master-mason was a man of some education, that he travelled all over Europe, as far as Hungary, and that he was interested in all forms of the building art from details of figure sculpture to the planning of an elaborate chevet with its vaulting and radiating chapels. He also gave designs for various machines to assist in building or in ingenious contrivances such as one to make an angel turn its head. The men who planned the great cathedrals must have had considerable knowledge of engineering in stone and mathematics, and were also sometimes called upon to keep accounts.

At Amiens and Reims the names of the master-masons were given the honour of having their names inscribed beside that of the bishop in the labyrinth placed on the floor of the nave, and Jean de Chelles signed his name in an inscription at the base of the transept of Notre-Dame, Paris. We are thus able to give the credit for the design of the nave of Amiens to Robert de Luzarches, of Reims to Jean d'Orbais, whose work was subsequently carried on by Jean Leloup, Gaucher de Reims and Bernard de Soissons.

The master-mason was treated as a gentleman, given a robe of office and entertained at the high table. He was provided with a house and sometimes with horses. A tomb-slab of Hue Libergier, the master of the destroyed thirteenth-century church of Saint-Nicaise at Reims, is still preserved in the cathedral, and depicts him in cap and robes of office, holding a model of a church and measuring rod in his hands, with his square and another tool placed in the corners.

The most distinguished of the master-masons were those who worked for the king, like Pierre de Montereau who rebuilt Saint-Denis in the third quarter of the thirteenth century, and who was employed on the tombs of the kings. Such men were in close personal touch with their master, and as time went on, especially in the new society which was forming after the Black Death and the wars of the fourteenth century, there was a tendency for them to become court officials, to be consulted about all the works undertaken by the monarch whether church, palace, castle or fortifications. Such a man was Raymond du Temple, master of the works to King Charles V and of Notre-Dame, Paris, at the end of the fourteenth century, or the sculptor Jean de Cambrai, who held the office of valet-de-chambre to the Duke of Burgundy in the fifteenth.

At the end of our period, by the beginning of the sixteenth century, conditions were beginning to show more signs of approximating to modern methods. When we read that Martin Chambiges, the celebrated Parisian architect, provided designs for the façade of Troyes and the transept fronts of Beauvais and Sens, it is difficult to believe that he could have given his personal superintendence to such diverse buildings, and must take it that he provided more elaborate designs than those made by the earlier working masons.

SHORT SELECTED BIBLIOGRAPHY

GENERAL

Sir Thomas G. Jackson. *Byzantine and Romanesque Architecture* (2 vols).
—— *Gothic Architecture* (2 vols). (Well illustrated with photographs and the author's beautiful drawings.)
A. W. Clapham. *Romanesque Architecture in Western Europe.* (A very valuable summary of recent research, with photographs and a useful series of plans.)
A. Kingsley Porter. *Medieval Architecture* (2 large vols). (Contains much information as to dating and descriptions of individual buildings.)
G. H. West. *Gothic Architecture in England and France.* (Interesting comparisons of contemporary work in the two countries.)
W. R. Lethaby. *Medieval Art.* (A very suggestive book—accounts of masons, etc.)
J. Baum. *Romanesque Architecture in France.* (An album of splendid photographs with brief introduction.)
R. de Lasteyrie. *L'Architecture Religieuse en France à l'Époque Romane.*
—— *L'Architecture Religieuse en France à l'Époque Gothique* (2 vols). (These are the most comprehensive works on the subject written with authority.)
C. Enlart. *Manuel de l'Archéologie Française.*
J. Puig-i-Cadafalch. *Le Premier Art Roman.*
J. A. Brutails. *Pour Comprendre les Monuments de la France.* (A monument of compression—illustrated by many small pictures.)
A. Michel. *Histoire de l'Art.* (A great work in many volumes, containing chapters by various authorities on architecture and the allied arts.)
Viollet-le-Duc. *Dictionnaire Raisonné de l'Architecture Française.* (A pioneer work on which most of the subsequent books have been based. Though much progress has been made in our knowledge since it was compiled, it remains a standard work and is an astonishingly good production for its date.)
The various monographs of the most important churches in France, especially the series "Petites Monographies des Grands Édifices de la France", published by H. Laurens, Paris. Also many valuable articles in French archaeological periodicals, especially the *Bulletin Monumental.*

SCULPTURE

A. Gardner. *Medieval Sculpture in France.* (With over 600 photographs.)
Marcel Aubert. *La Sculpture Française du Moyen Âge et de la Renaissance.* (A useful summary on a moderate scale.)
Marcel Aubert. *La Sculpture Française, 1140–1225* ⎫
P. Deschamps. *French Romanesque Sculpture* ⎬ sumptuous volumes issued by the Pegasus Press
P. Vitry. *French Sculpture during the Reign of* ⎪
St Louis, 1226–1270 ⎭
L. Lefrançois-Pillion. *Les Sculpteurs Français du XIIᵉ Siècle.*
—— *Les Sculpteurs Français du XIIIᵉ Siècle.*
A. Kingsley Porter. *Romanesque Sculpture of the Pilgrimage Roads.* (A very expensive work with 9 volumes of plates. A suggestive work challenging accepted theories of dating and in some cases carrying conviction.)
A. Humbert. *La Sculpture sous les Ducs de Bourgogne.*

85

BIBLIOGRAPHY

E. Houvet. *La Cathédrale de Chartres*. (Several volumes of superb photographs illustrating every detail of the sculpture and glass of the Cathedral.)
P. Vitry and G. Brière. *Documents de Sculpture Française du Moyen Âge*. (A great album of photographs—many from casts in the Trocadero.)

RECORDS

V. Mortet. *Recueil de Textes relatifs à l'histoire de l'Architecture et la condition des architectes*. Vol. i, XIe–XIIe siècles. Vol. ii, XIIe–XIIIe siècles.

ICONOGRAPHY

E. Mâle. *L'Art Religieux du XIIe Siècle*.
—— *L'Art Religieux du XIIIe Siècle*.
—— *L'Art Religieux de la fin du Moyen Âge*.

ARCHITECTS AND MASONS

H. Stein. *Les Architectes des Cathédrales Gothiques*.
M. Bauchal. *Nouveau Dictionnaire des Architectes Français*.
D. Knoop and D. P. Jones. *The Medieval Mason*. (A critical survey based on English records, but conditions were doubtless very similar in France.)
Album de Villard de Honnecourt. Reproduced in facsimile.

PLATES

1. POITIERS   Baptistery (or Temple) Saint-Jean

This is one of the few buildings in France which can be reasonably assigned to Merovingian
times. No records of its building exist, but it is generally supposed to have been erected
on the site of a Gallo-Roman hall at the end of the seventh century. It is built of
small stones and contains many Roman tiles and other older fragments. The oblong central
hall is timber-roofed and opens into apses on three sides, while the fourth, if it ever existed,
was replaced by a porch in the eleventh century. The walls are decorated with arcading,
and the exterior gables with triangular pediments and portions of pilasters. In spite of
considerable modern restoration, it remains a very interesting relic of this remote period.
(See also pl. 5 a.)

2. Venasque   Baptistery

This is assigned to the first quarter of the seventh century. In shape it has a general resemblance to that at Poitiers, but being smaller is entirely roofed in stone. Some of the columns and capitals may have been looted from Roman buildings. Our illustration shows the baptismal piscina in the centre.

3. JOUARRE   Crypt

This is believed to be the remains of a church built in 634. It contains a series of ancient tombs, of which one is that of an abbess who died in the middle of the seventh century. The high quality of the Corinthian and Composite capitals is remarkable at this date, and they have been regarded in some quarters as work of the fourth or fifth century re-employed. The columns and capitals are of marble. An extension was made in the tenth or eleventh century, which is of much coarser workmanship, and the groined vaulting over the whole probably dates from this period. The original part almost certainly had only a wooden roof at first.

4. GERMIGNY-DES-PRÉS   (a) Exterior   (b) Interior

Built by Theodulfus, Bishop of Orleans, and consecrated in 806. It consists of a square covered by a dome raised to form a square tower externally. This was surrounded by aisles and these opened into four apses, one of which was removed in the eleventh century to make room for the present nave. The church was famous for its rich decorations in stucco and mosaic, set up in emulation of Charlemagne's famous church at Aachen, but of these only the mosaic in the eastern apse survives.

This church was unfortunately drastically restored and almost rebuilt in 1867–70, when it lost much of its venerable appearance, and valuable evidences of its original design were obliterated.

5. (a) POITIERS   Baptistery Saint-Jean   (b) BEAUVAIS   Basse-Œuvre
Exterior

(a) See p. 2 and pl. 1.

(b) The eastern part was destroyed to make room for the vast Gothic choir, and the present portion owes its survival to the failure to complete the great church.

It is severely plain, with a wooden roof and no mouldings. Windows are round-headed, and the only ornament consists of simple patterns in brick.

This has usually been dated as begun in 987, but it has recently been shown that this record refers to another building. It is now believed to be a work of the eighth century.

93

6. VIENNE   Saint-Pierre

Founded in the fifth century, this church is believed to have been destroyed by the Saracens
in the eighth century. It was restored or rebuilt in the ninth and again in 924 and in the
eleventh and twelfth centuries. De Lasteyrie believed that the outer walls shown in our
illustration are the remains of the original fifth-century church, and that the present tall
plain arcade was built in the tenth century.

The church is now used as a museum.

7. Châtillon-sur-Seine   Saint-Vorles

Built about 991, with later additions.
  One of the earliest churches in France of the basilican type provided with transept and
central cupola.
  The flat buttresses, joined at the top by a shallow arcade—the so-called Lombard bands—
are characteristic of the "First Romanesque". (See ch. 1, p. 5.)

95

8. MONTMAJOUR   Oratory of St Trophime

Built to include the rock-hewn oratory of the saint, this little chapel has a very early appearance, but most experts do not think it can be dated earlier than the eleventh century. The capitals are roughly reminiscent of Classical types, and belong to the Carolingian tradition. M. Benoit, author of the monograph on Montmajour, considers it of tenth-century date, and we shall probably not be far wrong in dating it *c.* 1000.

9. MONTMAJOUR   Chapelle Sainte-Croix

Apparently a cemetery chapel, attached to the graveyard of the monastery, and dedicated in 1019. Its plan, consisting of four apses round a central space with an added porch, is referred to on pp. 9 and 12.

10. (a) LE PUY   Capital in cloister   (b) CHAMALIÈRES   Capital in narthex

(a) This famous cloister (see pl. 61) is of at least two dates. Most of it is of the twelfth century, but it incorporates work in one gallery which is assigned by Viollet-le-Duc to the tenth century and cannot be later than the beginning of the eleventh. This capital with its Ionic volutes is a good specimen of Carolingian work.

(b) This rudely-carved capital also suggests a Carolingian origin, and though the builders of the Auvergne churches seem to have been conservative in their methods, it is probable that the nave and narthex of this church may be assigned to the tenth century.

11. CRAVANT   Exterior

A good example of a Carolingian church dating probably from the tenth century.
   The design is of the simplest with a wooden roof. The characteristic feature is the masonry, mostly
of small stones with courses of different colours, or of brick or tiles, arranged in patterns. The round-
headed windows are like those in the Basse-Œuvre at Beauvais, and the triangular gables between them
are reminiscent of the Poitiers baptistery, and of Saxon work in England.

12. JUMIÈGES   Saint-Pierre

A ruin standing beside those of the great abbey church of the eleventh century. It seems
to have been built about 940. Its most remarkable feature is the triforium-gallery with
twin arches separated by a column, the ancestor of a very favourite type adopted by the
Romanesque builders of the following generations.

13. TOURNUS   Saint-Philibert

Exterior narthex and west end

This remarkable church—the largest and most imposing of the pre-Romanesque churches
in France—has been the object of much controversy. It was rebuilt 946–79 after destruction by the Huns, and there was another disastrous fire in 1008. The strange vault
and upper parts of the towers were added early in the twelfth century.

The two-storied narthex (for the interior see pl. 14) is built up into a great western
tower, divided later into two at the top, and provides excellent specimens of the Lombard
bands (see p. 5). M. Virey, the historian of the church, thinks this was built as a kind
of fortress after the disasters, and that the lower portion was put in hand by Abbot Aimin
who died in 946, but that the upper story was not completed before the end of the century.
Others, however, consider it all of one date as the exterior elevation does not correspond
with the interior division.

The west door was rebuilt in 1848.

14. Tournus   Interior of narthex

This shows the lower story with its groined vaults and heavy pillars, probably built by
946. The upper chamber has a barrel vault supported by quarter-circle vaults over the
aisles. It was originally approached by staircases from the aisles.

15. TOURNUS   Interior of nave

M. Virey thinks the enormous round piers were built by Abbot Bernier for the church
consecrated in 1019, which was then covered by a wooden roof. The remarkable vault
seems to have been added at the beginning of the twelfth century together with the inner
part of the apse, as there was another consecration in 1120.

   Heavy transverse arches were thrown across the nave from pillar to pillar, and on these
a series of short barrel vaults were erected at right angles to the axis of the building. These
allow of high windows, as the side walls have little constructional value, while each vault
resists the thrust of the next, the two end ones being supported by the great weight of the
towers. Mechanically the system was excellent, but for aesthetic reasons it was seldom
repeated except in the aisles, where it was frequently adopted by Cistercian churches, as
at Fontenay (pl. 77), and in our English Fountains.

16. Tournus   Ambulatory of choir

There is good evidence for the crypt being that completed in 979. If so it is an early example
of the ambulatory plan with radiating chapels. The chapels above are square-ended and
together with the outer walls of the ambulatory would seem to belong to the church of
1019. The columns of the sanctuary were rebuilt early in the twelfth century, and it is
probable that the annular vault with its rather clumsy transverse arches was built then
to join up with the new work.

17. Le Puy   Chapelle Saint-Michel d'Aiguilhe

This little chapel, perched on its astonishing pinnacle of rock, was founded in 963. It is
irregular in shape owing to the narrowness of the site. The irregular groined vaults resemble
those of some early crypts, and some of the capitals are Carolingian in type, but there may
have been some reconstruction in the twelfth century, when the remarkable doorway (see
pl. 62) was added.

18. Cruas   Exterior east end

This church has a square tower at the west end and a round one over the crossing. The walls of the nave and the apses have Lombard bands, but in spite of these early features the church is considered to be not earlier than the beginning of the twelfth century, and to be an instance of the survival of older ideals. It is built over a tenth-century crypt, and it looks as though the twelfth-century builders had to make allowances for the conservatism of those who had become used to the previous building. The fineness of the work is difficult to reconcile with an earlier date. Lombard bands tend to persist in Provence as on the tower at Arles (pl. 106a). The work is supposed to have been begun at the east end in 1098, but that the whole church was not finished till *c.* 1150.

19. (a) BERNAY   (b) CAEN   La Trinité (or Abbaye aux Dames)—aisle

(a) The earliest of the greater churches in Normandy, founded about 1013 and built under the direction of William of Volpiano. This has been quoted as evidence of the influence of Lombardy in starting the Norman school, but there is really little resemblance to any work in Lombardy or even Burgundy, and we must beware of regarding great ecclesiastics and patrons of the arts, to whom the honour is assigned of building these churches, as in any sense architects. The plan is very simple, with a wooden roof in the middle and groined vaults in the aisles. The arches are of several orders, with semi-columns to carry the innermost, which is rounded. We have here the germ of the system of articulation described on p. 21.

(b) Founded 1064 by Matilda, queen of William the Conqueror. Crypt, choir and aisles are of her date, but the upper parts of the nave were remodelled when the vault was added in the middle of the twelfth century. The old groined vaults of the aisles, now considerably distorted, are well shown in our illustration.

20. (a) SAVENNIÈRES   (b) SAINT-GEORGES-DE-BOSCHERVILLE
Transept

(a) A good example of a Carolingian church, tenth century (?). The porch is, of course, later. The chief feature is the masonry of small stones with courses of tiles arranged to form patterns.

(b) Founded in the last half of the eleventh century, this church appears to have been rebuilt in the early twelfth. Vaulting was added in the thirteenth, and the thickness of the walls has withstood the thrust without extra buttressing. The gallery across the end of the transept is a Norman feature, repeated at Winchester, etc.

21. REIMS   Saint-Rémi

This famous church, as it stood before the Great War, was a composite building of various dates. The original nave and transepts dated from 1038–49, and the main arcade and triforium belonged to this. A radical reconstruction took place *c.* 1170–90, when the early Gothic choir was built and the wooden roof of the nave was replaced by a stone vault. Extra pillars were placed against the old piers to support the new vaulting shafts, and the whole effect was altered. This vault over the nave was replaced last century by a wood and plaster imitation, as it had become dangerous, and this in turn collapsed entirely in the bombardment during the War, though sufficient of the stone vault of the choir survived to make restoration possible.

The choir, which was probably the first part undertaken *c.* 1170, is one of the most charming of the early Gothic style. It retains the roomy tribunes of the Romanesque period, with a little triforium above, and the groups of lancets forming the clerestory seem to be a special feature in Champagne, and may be compared with the very similar choir of Notre-Dame, Chalons-sur-Marne (pl. 123). The exterior of the apse is supported by some of the earliest flying buttresses in France (pl. 122).

22. MONTIER-EN-DER   Nave

Consecrated in 998.

Very plain with no carved ornament. In general outline must have been very like the first state of Saint-Rémi at Reims.

A fine early thirteenth-century choir was added later.

23. VIGNORY   Nave

This church is very similar in style to that at Montier-en-Der, and has been claimed as Carolingian in date, but a record exists that it was only recently completed in 1050. Unless it had been a long time building, it is probably a case of a conservative retention of a type rapidly growing out of fashion.

24. JUMIÈGES   Nave

Built 1040–67, this is one of the earliest of the great Norman churches, and shows the state of architecture in Normandy in the period immediately preceding the Conquest of England.

It has the usual three-story elevation, and the alternate bay design. Shafts rise from the alternate piers to the roof, although vaulting does not seem to have been intended. It has been suggested that they supported transverse stone arches intended to bind the building together and form a base for a wooden roof, like the scheme adopted at San Miniato at Florence.

25. CAEN   Saint-Étienne (Abbaye aux Hommes)—façade

Founded by William the Conqueror *c.* 1064 and dedicated in 1077. The west front, the oldest part, is very simple in design and remains in its original condition, with the exception of the upper parts of the towers, and the spires—the latter added at the end of the twelfth century.

26. CAEN   Saint-Étienne—interior from west

The Conqueror's church has been much altered, and a new choir added at the beginning
of the thirteenth century. There is no record of the date when the present vault replaced
the original wooden ceiling, but it was probably before the middle of the twelfth century.
It is a good example of sexpartite vaulting, which was widely adopted in the latter part of
the century, and exported to Canterbury. It is well adapted to the alternate bay system
(see p. 16), as two bays are grouped into a space nearly square, and the diagonal ribs are
brought down to the major piers, while an extra rib is brought up to the centre from the
shaft carried up from the minor piers. These vaulting shafts and other alterations were,
no doubt, added when the vault was erected.

114

27. CAEN   Saint-Étienne—bay scheme of nave

This photograph shows the alterations more clearly than the general view. The roomy
tribunes are covered with half-barrel vaults to abut the main vault.

   The parapets are, of course, later—probably fourteenth-century. The clerestory with a
tall central arch containing a window, flanked by two short arches separated by columns,
is the characteristic Norman scheme, but here one of the side arches has been removed in
each bay to make room for the vaulting ribs. The arches were probably originally square cut,
and the mouldings added during the reconstruction.

28. CAEN   La Trinité (Abbaye aux Dames)

Founded by Matilda, queen of William the Conqueror, *c.* 1062, and consecrated 1072. It preserves the original choir and an interesting crypt beneath it, while the groined vaults of the aisles survive (see pl. 19 b). A sexpartite vault was added to the nave *c.* 1140, and the west front probably dates from that time.

29. BEAUVAIS   Saint-Étienne—south aisle of nave

The nave appears to date from the first quarter of the twelfth century, with some later
alterations to the main vault, etc. A sixteenth-century choir completes the building.

The aisle-vaults are an excellent example of the difficulties which the masons had to face
while still retaining the round arch. In order to keep the crown of the vault approximately
level the transverse arches are stilted, rising perpendicularly from the capital for some way
before the curve begins, while the diagonals are made rather less than semicircles, and rise
at a very awkward angle from their capitals. Such difficulties were later overcome by the
introduction of the pointed arch, which can be adapted to any shape required, and at the
same time exercises less thrust.

30. BAYEUX   Nave arcade

One of the richest twelfth-century arcades in France. The lavish use of mouldings is characteristic of Normandy, and is a distinguishing mark of the local style during the next century as well. In this Normandy is nearer to English fashions than to the rest of France.

The strange carvings in the little niches between the arches are almost Chinese in character, and show the poor quality of figure-sculpture here as compared with geometric patterns or foliage. They may be relics of the eleventh-century church.

The late eleventh-century church was burnt by Henry I of England in 1105, and its remains are encased in the later piers. Another fire caused a reconstruction after 1160, from which time we may date the rich carving of the arcades. Again, in the early years of the thirteenth century, the aisles were rebuilt and vaulted, and it seems probable that the inner order with its advanced capitals was then added to strengthen the building. The upper part with the windows and vault is fine work of the middle of the thirteenth century.

31. MORIENVAL   (a) North aisle of nave   (b) Ambulatory

(a) The original church, of which the north aisle is the most genuine portion, appears to be a work of the second half of the eleventh century, and the groined vault, though restored, must follow the old lines.

(b) The eastern part of the church seems to have been rebuilt about 1122, and is remarkable for the very narrow ambulatory with its clumsy ribbed vaults, which are among the earliest noted in France. Far more accomplished vaults of the new type appeared between 1130 and 1140, and Dr J. Bilson has shown good reason to date the Durham vaults considerably earlier. It looks therefore as though Morienval was a local experiment on the new plan rather than a pioneer enterprise.

32. NEVERS   Cathedral—western apse

Like many German churches, Nevers has an apse at the west as well as the east end. It is
of eleventh-century date and opens into a western transept, beyond which is the early
fourteenth-century church on a normal plan.

The double apsed plan was adopted in the Saxon cathedral at Canterbury.

33. SAINT-BENOÎT-SUR-LOIRE   Narthex

The ancient abbey at Fleury rose to great fame when the relics of St Benedict were brought there from Monte Cassino in 655.

The great porch-tower which precedes the nave is most imposing, although incomplete at the top. It was begun by Abbot Gauzlin (1004–29), but work was interrupted by a fire, and the present edifice appears to be mainly work of the second half of the eleventh century.

34. SAINT-BENOÎT-SUR-LOIRE   Choir

The choir was begun by Abbot William (1067–80) and was consecrated in 1108. The closely-placed pillars of the arcade with a blank wall above, no doubt originally painted, the shallow triforium arcade and smooth barrel vaults are all characteristic of the Loire Valley at this early date.

Like Cluny this great church has a double transept, and the nave seems to have been added in a more leisurely manner through a great part of the twelfth century, the vaults probably having been finished before another dedication in 1218.

35. SAINT-GENOU   Choir arcade

Another eleventh-century church, with a choir separating the nave from the apse. The choir-arcade, seen here from the aisle, has extraordinarily massive columns with huge quaintly-carved capitals, and the general effect is almost more like an Indian temple than a French church.

36. ANGOULÊME   Façade
(a) Central portion—present condition   (b) Before restoration (from a very old
                                                   photograph)
                                          (Kindly lent by Mr P. M. Johnston, F.S.A.)

The cathedral at Angoulême suffered a disastrous restoration by Abadie in 1866–75, when the upper
part was renewed from his own designs. Much of the sculpture spread over the whole front, representing
a kind of mixture between the Ascension and the Second Coming, is mainly original, though no doubt
touched up. Reference to the old photograph shows the central door with its tympanum to be a
restoration, probably incorrect, as large tympanum carvings are rare in the south-west. The smaller
ones at the side in the blank arcades unpierced by doorways are characteristic of the style.
   The cathedral was begun c. 1105 and consecrated in 1128.

37. Saint-Amand-de-Boixe   West wall of transept

This church, consecrated in 1170, used to be taken as an argument for dating the sculptures of Angoulême and much of the western sculpture half a century too late. Its close resemblance to Angoulême is obvious, but a cursory examination of the church shows that this is part of an older building incorporated in an enlarged church of late Romanesque character. Now Prof. Kingsley Porter has found an earlier consecration of Saint-Amand in 1125, and shown that the later church was that consecrated in 1170. If we accept the 1125 date, it agrees closely with the recorded consecration of Angoulême in 1128, which had been rejected for the sake of a theory thus proved false.

38. (a) SAINTES   Saint-Eutrope   (b) SOUILLAC

126

38. (a) SAINTES   Saint-Eutrope

(a) A good example of a south-western type church, with lofty arcades covered with a barrel vault with solid transverse arches. The aisles too are lofty to allow of light from their windows to enter the central nave, and they are covered with half-barrel vaults to resist the thrust of the heavy nave vault (see pl. 51 b).

The crypt is believed to date 1096 and the upper church must have followed shortly after.

(b) SOUILLAC

(b) A good example of the wide nave covered by a series of flat domes resting on very heavy transverse arches, and pendentives (see p. 19). Unlike Byzantine domes there is no drum between the base and curved part of the dome. There has been considerable controversy over the dates of these domed churches, but it is now believed that several of them were rebuilt in this form well on in the twelfth century owing to the failure of the original barrel vaults.

39. CHARROUX   Rotunda

This remarkable ruin is all that remains of an important church consecrated in 1096. The central portion formed a rotunda carried up to form a tower, and was surrounded by a double aisle. The plan seems to have been copied from that of Saint-Benigne at Dijon, built by William of Volpiano c. 1000.

40. PÉRIGUEUX   Saint-Front

A great controversy has raged about the date of this celebrated building, which has been
made all the more confused by the drastic restoration by Abadie, which amounted almost
to rebuilding. It consists of two parts, the remains of an older church of basilican form at
the west end, and a huge centrally planned cross church roofed by five domes, closely
resembling St Mark's at Venice, as built in the mid-eleventh century, from which Saint-
Front is supposed to have been inspired. The most probable theory is that the western
bays are what survived of the church consecrated in 1047, which was burnt in 1120, and
that the domed church was the result of the rebuilding after the fire.

41. SOLIGNAC   Interior

Another good example of the domed type. The four arches supporting the domes are
extremely solid, and an arcade runs along the outer walls with a shelf above it under the
windows, while a narrow passage through the great piers allows room for cleaners or
others to walk round at this level. In this case the domes do not show from outside, being
hidden under a continuous wooden outer roof.

Consecrated 1143. The use of the pointed arch suggests a twelfth-century date; though
it was employed for constructional purposes in Burgundy at the end of the eleventh century,
and still earlier in the east, it was not in common use in the west quite so early.

130

42. CAHORS   Cathedral interior

One of the oldest of these domed churches, consecrated in 1119. The eastern part was remodelled in the fourteenth century. Outside the domes are uncovered and give a very Oriental effect. The domes of the first quarter of the twelfth century seem to have been constructed of concrete, those of the middle of the century of shaped stone.

Cahors is of vast proportions, being some 65 feet in width, and the idea of a great cave-like hall undivided by pillars seems to have appealed to the imagination, especially of these southern districts.

43. LOCHES   (a) Exterior   (b) Interior

This strange church seems to be a northern version of the domed scheme, but instead of dome sit has a series of hollow spires, composed of narrowing courses of stone without any thrust. Externally the church appears to consist of four steeples in a row, with an apse at one end, and a porch at the other. There has been a good deal of restoration, but the present form seems to have good authority. The whole of the upper part of the steeples was rebuilt *c.* 1853.

These strange pyramids were the work of Prior Thomas who died in 1168 towards the end of his life. They then replaced a wooden roof which covered the old eleventh-century church.

44. POITIERS   Notre-Dame-la-Grande—façade

The most elaborate of the south-western façades, with every inch covered with sculpture. There is no tympanum over the doorway, and only the central arch is pierced for a door. The scaled spires of the corner turrets are characteristic of this district.

The date is not recorded, but the front is probably a work of the second quarter of the twelfth century.

133

45. CIVRAY   Façade

Another example of these rich south-western façades. The sculpture is spread over the whole front, instead of being confined to the porches, and is perhaps more effective from its mass than from the distinction of its individual pieces. The tympanum over the doorway is a modern insertion, and is probably a mistaken restoration, as such things are rare in this part of France. The statues placed in the upper arches do not appear to be in their original positions in every case. There is a record of a church here in 1119, but the façade certainly looks more like a work of the middle of the century, unless falsified by the restoration of 1845.

134

46. AULNAY   South transept

This is a remarkable example of the richness of decoration of the south-western school. and
is of special interest to the student of sculpture. The south transept with its doorway appears
to be the oldest part, *c.* 1120–30, while the west front must be work of the second half of
the twelfth century.

47. AULNAY   South transept doorway

One of the richest examples of the elaborate carving of this district, probably *c.* 1120–30. The concentric rings of carving—the 24 Elders multiplied to fill the space, and a strange collection of beasts and monsters—are arranged to radiate from the centre, while in the later doorway at the west the figures stand one above another as in the Gothic porches of the next period.

There is no tympanum, and the sculpture is remarkable more for quantity than quality.

136

48. AULNAY   Apse

Decoration in these churches is applied to the apse as well as the façade. The column-buttresses with carved capitals and head-corbels under the eaves give a very rich effect. Shallow scroll-work is carried right round the east window.

49. AULNAY   Interior

A good example of the interior of one of these south-western churches. They are of no
great height, and are covered by a pointed barrel vault, with strengthening transverse
arches, and no direct lighting of the nave apart from the west window and from the aisles.
There is a kind of dome under the central tower, and a plain apse without pillars or
ambulatory.

138

50. CUNAULT   Interior of apse

This church near the Loire has close affinities with those farther south. We have here an apse with a very narrow ambulatory separated from the sanctuary by tall clustered columns supporting stilted arches, and with carved capitals. There is a pointed barrel vault.

Date probably second quarter of the twelfth century, with the exception of the western bays of the nave, built *c.* 1200.

51. (a) MELLE   Saint-Hilaire—aisle   (b) SAINTES   Saint-Eutrope—aisle

These show the very narrow aisles of the south-western school, with vaults raised almost as high as those of the central nave, allowing some light from the windows in the outside wall to penetrate into the middle of the church. In that from Saintes we have the earlier plan in which a half-barrel vault is used to resist the pressure of the nave-vault, and in that from Melle a pointed barrel scheme is adopted, both being strengthened by heavy transverse arches.

52. SAINTES   Notre-Dame—west doorway

An astonishing example of the wealth of barbaric carving lavished on these south-western doorways.
There is no tympanum, but the numerous orders of the arch are covered with sculpture. Each
voussoir is carved separately, usually with one figure, and they are placed radially round the arch.
Owing to this peculiarity the subjects are difficult to identify: in the fourth row from outside, for
example, the Massacre of the Holy Innocents is disguised by allotting one voussoir to each soldier and
one to each baby, with the result that soldiers and babies are the same size, and the whole scene looks
more like a battle.

Date, early twelfth century. The abbey was founded in 1047, but the façade cannot be so early
as that.

53. MELLE   Saint-Pierre—exterior of apse

An example of the tri-apsidal plan, with smaller apses ending the aisles on each side of the central one. The pillar buttresses and richly decorated windows give a sumptuous effect. Windows are still round-headed though in constructional features such as the vault and main arcade the pointed arch is used.

Date, second quarter of twelfth century.

54. MELLE   Saint-Hilaire—exterior of apse

Here we have a more elaborate plan with an ambulatory, out of which five apsidal chapels
open. The eastern portion was built in the first half of the twelfth century, and the nave
rather later.

143

55. SAINTES   Saint-Eutrope—subsidiary apsidal chapel

Another rich example of the south-western school. Blank arcading at the top and a carved
string-course lower down add to the effect.

The buttress system of the nave walls with a series of arches springing from columns and
enclosing the windows can be seen here. A similar arrangement was illustrated at Aulnay
(pl. 46).

56. AIRVAULT   West porch

This large porch, almost comparable to the Burgundian "narthex", provides a stately
entrance to the church. The large capitals and massive columns indicate a fairly early
date, which makes the attribution to Abbot Peter who is said to have built the church, and
who died in 1110, a fairly safe one.

57. ISSOIRE   Exterior

A typical Auvergne church. Note especially the octagonal tower supported by two lofty
bays on each side over the transept, producing a pyramidal effect. The decoration round
the main apse, and elsewhere, by a kind of coarse mosaic pattern of light and dark stone
is also characteristic of this school.

The apse with ambulatory and radiating chapels made an early appearance in the
Auvergne, the foundations of the old cathedral at Clermont of 946 showing the earliest
example noted in France. In one or two cases the eastern chapel is omitted, or made
square-ended as here.

The chronology of the Auvergne churches has been much disputed, but the latest
opinion is that none of the existing specimens are earlier than the twelfth century. The
actual tower itself is a nineteenth-century reconstruction, like several of those in Auvergne.

58. CLERMONT-FERRAND   Notre-Dame-du-Port—interior

Another typical Auvergne church. The plain round barrel vault without transverse arches,
the absence of mouldings on the arches, the triforium with half-barrel vaults and absence
of any clerestory lighting give a primitive look to these churches. The general design carries
on that of eleventh-century buildings like Conques, but there is reason to believe that they
are not earlier than the middle of the twelfth century and that the retention of older forms
is a mark of the conservatism of this mountain region. There is a record of work of some
kind still going on at Notre-Dame-du-Port as late as 1185.

147

59. SAINT-NECTAIRE   Interior

A smaller, but similar design to that of Clermont. The choir is lower than the nave, but the
tower raised on squinches above the Auvergnat transept is so high that a window into it is
inserted over the main arch across the end of the nave.

Probable date, 1146–78. The upper part of the tower was rebuilt in 1876.

148

60. SAINT-NECTAIRE   Ambulatory

Has a simple groined vault. The capitals round the sanctuary are very large, and elaborately
carved with figure subjects. There is a family likeness between the capitals at Clermont,
Saint-Nectaire, Issoire and Mozac which indicates that all must be of approximately
similar date. The finest include one now on the floor at Mozac which has a quality which
cannot be assigned to an earlier date than the second half of the twelfth century.

149

61. Le Puy   Cloister

The buildings at Le Puy have a character of their own, which distinguishes them from the
Auvergne group, though they have some features in common, such as the use of dark and
light stone alternately, as in this cloister. This cloister is of two dates, the earlier portion
being of the tenth or eleventh century (see the capital pl. 10a), and the later of the twelfth
century. This part is of an unusually solid design, and some of the capitals are of so peculiar
a character that one is tempted to suggest Moorish influence, which is in evidence here in
other ways.

62. Le Puy   Saint-Michel l'Aiguilhe—doorway

This elaborate doorway is a later addition to the early chapel illustrated in pl. 17. It suggests Eastern or Moorish influence in the huge cusping of the trefoil arch, the flat carving and the mosaic inlay in coloured stones.

(b) PARAY-LE-MONIAL   Interior

63. (a) CLUNY

63. (a) CLUNY

(a) A single transept crowned by an octagonal tower,·and flanked by a smaller bell-tower, is all that is left of what was in its day the largest church in Christendom. The greater part, no doubt damaged at the Revolution, was destroyed in 1811.

This fragment was part of the church built by St Hugh and begun 1089. It was consecrated in 1095 and again in 1131, the second time probably after the repairs to the nave caused by the collapse of the vault in 1125. The whole church including the narthex added c. 1220 was about 560 feet long, and the nave vault over 98 feet high. There were double aisles, double transept and seven towers. There was a pointed barrel vault, and the arches of the arcades were also pointed. The splendid capitals of the sanctuary have been recovered and placed in the local museum; they show very skilful sculpture for a date before 1095.

(b) PARAY-LE-MONIAL   Interior

(b) Built at the same time as the great church at Cluny, this may serve to give some idea of the style of the greater church. The ambulatory plan, pointed barrel vault boldly raised high enough to allow of clerestory windows, and fluted pilasters help to make this a useful example of Cluniac architecture in Burgundy c. 1100.

64. VÉZELAY   Interior of nave

64. VÉZELAY   Interior of nave

This famous abbey was placed under Cluny at the period of the building of the present church, but the style is very different from that of its great rival. It is much lower, and the round arch is retained throughout. Heavy transverse arches, composed of dark and light stones alternately, are thrown across the nave, and support a groined vault—a form usually reserved for the aisles, but allows of direct lighting by clerestory windows. There is no triforium. The sculpture of the doorways and capitals is very remarkable.

There was a consecration in 1104, but this may have been only of the choir, later replaced by the late twelfth-century choir we now see (pl. 159). It seems likely, however, that the nave was built before 1120, when some damage was done by fire and smoke. The later narthex, which has pointed arches, was consecrated in 1132.

65. Paray-le-Monial   Exterior

The nave is very short, partly owing to the wish of the builders of *c.* 1100 to preserve the
narthex and western towers of the older church, presumably that consecrated in 1004.
The upper part of the north tower, however, must belong to the later reconstruction. The
central tower is only a restoration of 1860; the old tower had been rebuilt in the fourteenth
century, and was becoming ruinous.

156

66. Autun Cathedral   Interior of nave

A good example of twelfth-century Burgundian style. Pointed arches, and pointed barrel
vault raised high enough to allow of clerestory windows, form a bold composition, but one
which had subsequently to be propped up by flying buttresses. The capitals are interesting,
and the fluted pilasters and triforium, copied from the still remaining Roman gate of the
city, give it a very Classical appearance.

The cathedral was begun in 1119, and consecrated in 1132 and again in 1146.

67. AUTUN   West porch

Instead of a closed-in narthex Autun has a large porch of two bays with a grand stair leading up
to the doorway. Over the door is the vast tympanum with its strangely elongated figures and fearsome
devils, features strongly characteristic of monastic Burgundy.

158

68. (a) LA CHARITÉ-SUR-LOIRE (b) AUTUN   Bay of choir
   Junction of choir and transept

(a) In general the bay scheme follows the Burgundian plan, as at Autun, but treatment is simpler and the Classical features less prominent. The triforium has lobed arches, which are thought to derive ultimately from Moorish sources. The transept with its absolutely plain eastern chapels appears to be earlier work not later than the eleventh century.

(b) Shows clearly the fluted pilasters and almost Roman details, apart from the use of the pointed arch.

69. LA CHARITÉ   Interior of apse

This broad ring of columns with narrow arches and bold carved capitals forms a most imposing termination to the great church.

70. LA CHARITÉ   Exterior apse and tower

This great apse with its ring of chapels, the long transept, and fine octagonal tower form a
grand composition. The western bays of the nave are in ruins, but one of the western towers
survives.

71. NEVERS   Saint-Étienne—interior

This fine early church, consecrated in 1097, is usually classed with the Burgundian group,
though it has affinities with eleventh-century churches elsewhere. The double-arched
tribunes resemble those of Conques, or the Auvergne, but the clerestory windows and lofty
barrel vault are those of Burgundy.

72. NEVERS   Saint-Étienne—exterior

The apse with ambulatory and radiating apsidal chapels is well developed, and the string-course with billet moulding over the windows and blind arcade under the eaves produce a fine decorative effect. In view of the solid construction, the flat early type of buttresses seem to have proved sufficient.

73. SEMUR-EN-BRIONNAIS   Doorway

An example of the extremely rich carving of the Burgundian doorways in the second half
of the twelfth century. The large relief in the tympanum is usual there, and the capitals of
modified Classical type, but in this case the pilasters have substituted more elaborate
patterns for the Roman flutings. The pointed arch is being used by this time for ornamental
features like doorways as well as for constructional advantage.

74. AVALLON   Detail of west doors

A magnificent example of the elaborate foliage sculpture employed in Burgundy. The capitals are of the Classic type based on the acanthus, but the great rosettes of the arch-moulds are a distinct peculiarity of this province. They occur in earlier and simpler form at Vézelay, and in fragments from Cluny, etc.

75. BOURGES   Detail of lintel of north door

Another superb piece of Romanesque foliage. The scroll on the lintel might almost have come from the Forum at Rome.

The two Romanesque doorways incorporated in the great thirteenth-century cathedral belong to an earlier church of which no records exist. From the style they must be dated about the middle of the twelfth century, or slightly before.

166

76. SAINT-MENOUX   Interior of apse

Although on the borders of what is known as Burgundy, this church is a good example of
the latest Burgundian Romanesque, almost verging on the Transition. The stilted arches of
the curved portion are round, but the others are sharply pointed. The fluted pilasters and
Classical patterns are much in evidence.

167

77. Fontenay   Interior of nave

The earliest of the important Cistercian abbeys which has survived. It was begun *c.* 1139 and finished in 1147. The Cistercian movement was started as a reaction against the love of splendour of the Cluniacs, and demanded absolute simplicity in its buildings, which depend entirely on proportion and constructional features for their effect. At Fontenay (now in private possession but shown to visitors) the great empty church shows this simplicity in an extreme form. It is vaulted with the Burgundian pointed barrel vault with transverse arches and no clerestory. All the light comes from the grouped windows at the ends together with what filters through from the aisle-chapels. The east end is square and the capitals merely blocked out. The aisles are roofed with barrel vaults at right angles to the axis of the church and were originally walled up into a series of chapels, one to each bay, though connecting arches have now been pierced through the partition walls. This was a scheme frequently adopted by the Cistercians, and may be seen as far away as Fountains in England.

The church was to a great extent built at the cost of Everard (or Ebrard) bishop of Norwich, who was driven out of his diocese and retired to Fontenay in 1139, where he built himself a castle just outside the abbey precincts.

78. Fontenay   Cloister

The monastic buildings are well preserved here as well as the church, and the cloister round which they are grouped is a very beautiful one. It is interesting to compare its stern simplicity, depending for its effect entirely on constructional fitness with the richly carved Benedictine and Cluniac cloisters whose capitals were carved with figures and foliage and the monsters and grotesques which called forth the famous tirade of the Cistercian St Bernard.

The cloister dates from the latter part of the twelfth century.

79. (a) SAINT-RESTITUT   (b) MONTMAJOUR   Interior of apse
Interior, looking west

(a) Shows the interior scheme of a late twelfth-century Provençal nave, without aisles and few windows. There is a pointed barrel vault reinforced by heavy transverse arches of two orders without mouldings. A carved string-course is carried round the supports and little twisted shafts with Classical capitals are placed high up on them below the cornice.

(b) Begun 1117, but not complete till 1153, this great empty church stands over an interesting crypt. The false ribs of the apse are clearly seen. They are more ornamental than constructional; they are part of the walling, not a framework upon which the filling was erected, and so do not anticipate the Gothic vault.

80. ARLES   Saint-Trophime—nave

Consecrated 1152, the nave is a good example of Provençal style of the first half of the
twelfth century. The work is very plain, the shafts being square-cut with no mouldings,
and capitals are mere narrow blocks. Many of these churches are without aisles, and when
they exist they are very narrow, as here. A local peculiarity is seen in the little columns on
either side of the vaulting shafts just below the springing of the vault—almost the only
ornamental feature. Parts of the transept may be as early as *c.* 1000.

81. ARLES   Saint-Trophime—porch

This famous porch contrasts in the richness of its decoration with the plain interior. Prof. Kingsley
Porter considered it part of the church consecrated in 1152, but French authorities like Comte de
Lasteyrie dated it *c.* 1180–90, taking as evidence the later form of mitre worn by one of the statues.
The design is based on Classical models, many of which of Roman date still survive in the district.
The statues and reliefs seem inspired by the sculptured sarcophagi, of which there are many in the
museum, but the crouching beasts under them connect with Lombard work. The capitals and scrolls
based on the Corinthian order are very well executed.

82. SAINT-GILLES   Porch

This porch—still more Classical in design than that at Arles—is a composite structure of two dates. The central part seems a little older than that at Arles, apart from the tympanum, which is a much later fakement, but the two outer bays appear to be considerably later. The Classical details of the capitals, etc., are exceedingly fine, but the strangely contorted attitudes of some of the larger figures are less Roman and more like the work in Languedoc. An inscription gives the date of the beginning of the work in the crypt as 1116, and there is reason to believe it finished c. 1140. The porch would therefore have been begun about the middle of the century.

83. Saint-Paul-Trois-Châteaux   Interior

A good example of a Provençal interior. In this case the barrel vault is round, not pointed, but it is doubtful whether this means it is earlier than the pointed variety. There is a little more ornament in the upper story, where there is a small clerestory arcade separated by pilasters with the middle arch pierced for a window. The upper part of the shafts supporting the transverse arches is spirally fluted. Like other churches of the district, though a cathedral, it is on a comparatively small scale, very solidly built as good stone was abundant in this part, and the outer roofing was laid directly on the roof. There are the usual false ribs in the apse.

Date, mid-twelfth century.

84. (a) CAVAILLON   Exterior of apse   (b) LE THOR   Porch

(a) It is a common feature in Provence for the apse to be polygonal outside, but round within. The fluted shafts at the corners and Corinthian-type capitals give this a very Roman appearance.

(b) Some of the doorways in Provence are very Classical in type, with detail copied from ancient monuments still surviving there. This detail is often very delicately wrought. The gable above supported by fluted pilasters also looks very Roman.

Date, late twelfth century.

85. SAINT-RESTITUT   Doorway

Another doorway of extraordinarily Classical type. It would do almost equally well for the first or the seventeenth century, but appears really to be of the second half of the twelfth century. It is a very faithful copy of a Roman model.

86. Saint-Gabriel (near Arles)   Doorway

Here again we have an extraordinarily Classical work of the twelfth century—so much so
that it is possible some of the details are really Roman, looted from ancient buildings and
re-used, as is suggested by the way the fragments do not all correspond. The tympanum
over the door and the relief in the pediment show very crude figure carving in contrast
with the delicacy of the surrounding architectural setting.

178

87. ARLES   Saint-Trophime—cloister

This cloister is of various dates. The west gallery is thirteenth-century work, while the south was only begun in 1389, but the north and east are twelfth-century work with barrel vaults and round arches. The north is the older and contains the finest sculpture. Comte de Lasteyrie, after an exhaustive analysis of the arguments and examination of the inscriptions, decided that it was completed c. 1180, and that the east gallery, shown in our picture, with its moulded arches, was slightly later. The Apostle on the right of our illustration is on the corner of the north gallery and belongs to the older work.

(a)

(b)

88. ARLES

Cloister—capitals

88. ARLES   Cloister—capitals

         (a) in north gallery   (b) in east gallery

These show the skill with which the Arles sculptors of the end of the twelfth century copied antique models. The rosettes, scrolls and acanthus leaves might almost pass as Roman work, but in the later series (in (b)) the foliage begins to show a more naturalistic touch, and the figure work in the Entry into Jerusalem is typically medieval, working out its own methods instead of copying the past.

181

89. VAISON   Cloister

This is a good example of the charming late twelfth-century cloisters of Provence. The grouping of three or more small arches on coupled shafts under a wide flat containing arch is repeated in a number of other cloisters, as at Montmajour, Saint-Rémy and Aix. The thickening given by the containing arches and the heavy piers separating each group of arcading are required to support the heavy stone vaulting. There has been much restoration.

Part of the walls seem to be of the eleventh century, but the arches and pillars belong to a reconstruction of c. 1200.

90. TOULOUSE   Saint-Sernin—interior

One of the great churches of the pilgrimage route. It is nobly planned, on a big scale with double aisles. There are roomy tribunes but no clerestory windows. There is a round barrel vault with transverse arches. The church is mainly built of brick, and the piers of the nave being merely plastered and painted in stone colour, the general effect is less imposing than in the other two great churches of this type at Conques and Santiago de Compostela, but this may have been less felt when they were built as there was then no doubt a much more lavish use of colour than modern taste approves.

The choir and transepts were begun c. 1077 and consecrated in 1096. The nave was finished apart from the vault in 1118, and there was a consecration in 1119. The church is believed to have been completed by 1124.

91. TOULOUSE   Saint-Sernin—tribunes of south transept

This is part of the church consecrated in 1096. The capitals are carved with foliage, beasts, birds and other figures. This group of churches, which included the destroyed church of Saint-Martial at Limoges, and is thought to have been inspired by Saint-Martin of Tours, has strongly developed transepts with aisles on both sides and across the ends, besides the usual ambulatory round the apse with its radiating chapels.

92. SANTIAGO DE COMPOSTELA   Interior of nave

Although far away in Spain the great cathedral at the end of the Pilgrimage is so much like
its French counterparts that it seems suitable to include it here. It has not the double aisles
of Toulouse, but the general scheme is the same, while the finer material and carved
capitals make it more impressive. The transepts have no less than six bays each, with aisles
all round, and though the late choir enclosure projecting into the nave, in accordance with
Spanish custom, cuts into the general view, it is less obtrusive than is usually the case in that
country. The famous Portico de la Gloria, carved by Master Mateo between 1168 and
1188, at the western end, is the supreme masterpiece of southern Romanesque sculpture.
    The great church was begun in 1078, the choir was finished in 1102 and the nave in 1124.

93. CONQUES   Sainte-Foy—interior

Although on a smaller scale than Toulouse, with a single-aisled nave of only six bays instead of twelve, this church remains one of the most imposing creations of Romanesque art. It has the roomy tribunes, with no attempt to weaken the round barrel vault by clerestory windows, except in the apse, and the strongly projecting transepts with aisles on both sides, the ambulatory round the apse and radiating chapels, and the lantern-dome over the crossing supported on squinches containing statues, all combine to make an exceptionally fine eastern termination. When we add to this the romantic situation in a remote valley among high hills, the superb and splendidly preserved carving of the Last Judgment on the huge tympanum of the west door, and the treasure with its unrivalled collection of early pieces including the astonishing miracle-working golden image of Sainte-Foy entirely encrusted with gems and precious stones and dating probably *c.* 950, an expedition to Conques becomes the most fascinating pilgrimage in all France for the modern antiquary.

Conques seems to have been begun by Abbot Odolric, 1030–65, and to have been finished *c.* 1100 apart from the west door and final touches. It is therefore slightly the earliest survivor of the eleventh-century group of great pilgrimage churches.

94. BEAULIEU (Corrèze)   Porch

Elaborate porches with a vast carved tympanum are a feature of a number of churches in
the Languedoc area. These seem to connect them with Burgundy rather than with Toulouse,
and the strange elongated and contorted figures are certainly more like those of Vézelay or
Autun than the short heavily proportioned figures of Toulouse or Santiago. This may be
due to Cluniac influence. The porch at Beaulieu is evidently inspired by that at Moissac,
which is believed to date from 1115, or soon after. We may therefore assume a date of
c. 1120–25 for it. There is another huge tympanum at Cahors, and a charming one, rather
smaller, at Carennac.

95. Saint-Aventin   Exterior from the east

This is an interesting twelfth-century church in a fine situation in a valley of the Pyrenees.
It has a central and a western tower, a fine south porch, and a central apse flanked by two
smaller ones. The flat buttresses and cornice of small arches on the apse are a reminiscence
of the Lombardic bands of the eleventh century. A number of sculptures of eleventh
century and earlier date have been built into the walls, and must have come from an older
church on this site.

96. (a) Saint-Paul-les-Dax   (b) Corneilla-de-Conflent
              Exterior of apse   Exterior of apse

Two examples of the external decoration of the apse in the Pyrenean district. That at Dax with its
elaborate arcade is more influenced by the south-western school to the north of it. The crude reliefs
set round it to form a frieze have been claimed as early work from some previous building, but their
adaptation to the curved surface of the apse seems to indicate that they were made for the position.

The apse at Corneilla-de-Conflent has a late version of the arcaded cornice, like that at Saint-
Aventin. The deeply recessed windows with openings little more than slits are typical of the south
where sunshine is looked upon more as an enemy than a friend.

97. MOISSAC   Cloister

A slab incorporated in one of the piers gives the date as 1100. It is disputed whether this merely refers to a number of marble slabs with figures of Apostles, of great interest for the study of early sculpture, or to the shafts and capitals as well, and there is also much controversy as to the relative dates of this cloister and that of Santo Domingo de Silos in Spain.

The upper part with the pointed arches is, of course, a later reconstruction in the Gothic period.

(a)

(b)

98. MOISSAC Cloister—capitals

98. MOISSAC   Cloister—capitals

(a) Foliage   (b) Figures—the Magi

These capitals show the extreme delicacy of the foliage and scroll-work contrasting with the primitive and elementary figure sculpture. If we accept the early date of 1100 for this work, it must be explained as due to Moorish influence. At that date Southern France and Northern Spain formed one art province, and the skill of the Moorish craftsmen in pattern-work must have had some influence on their Christian contemporaries. As, however, Moslems were forbidden to carve the figure, the twelfth-century masons had to work out their problems for themselves and their figure-work is much cruder than the foliage. Byzantine patterns seem to have reached the west through the Moors as well as by more direct routes.

193

99. ELNE   Cloister

The most elaborate French cloister after that at Arles. It is built of marble, and many of the shafts, as well as the capitals, are carved. It seems to have suffered considerable damage in a siege in 1285, and what we have now is a fourteenth-century reconstruction of the twelfth-century cloister. Most of the old shafts and capitals were used again, though there are a number which had to be recut or rather clumsily copied. The old round arches were retained, but a Gothic ribbed vault was added, and some of the thick square piers set at intervals to support it appear to be entirely of fourteenth-century design.

100. SAINT-BERTRAND-DE-COMMINGES   Cloister

This beautiful Pyrenean cloister is supposed to have been built by St Bertrand himself.
He died in 1123, but some of the capitals with their crocket-like foliage suggest a considerably later date. Possibly, as often happened in these parts, the construction was
spread over a long period, and only the older part actually dates from the time of the
founder. The honeycomb capitals seem to suggest Moorish influence, which is frequently
met with in the border country. In one bay figures of the four Evangelists placed back to
back replace the columns.

The cloister was in a ruinous condition, but has now been roofed in and is looked after.
It was never vaulted.

101. SAINT-LIZIER   Cloister

This beautiful cloister is lightly constructed, and was never vaulted. As at Moissac, single and double columns alternate. The capitals are all different, and show a great variety of Byzantine basket and interlacing patterns treated with freedom and mixed with figures and foliage of more Classical type. The work appears to be of the second half of the twelfth century. An upper story supported on plain wooden shafts was added at a much later period.

Moorish influence is felt in most of the Pyrenean cloisters, while Classical traditions are stronger in those of Provence.

102. Saint-Michel-de-Cuxa   Tower

This is the survivor of a pair of transeptal towers, the rest of the church being ruinous.
It was built in the last quarter of the tenth century, and a letter written in 1040 describes
it, though the towers do not appear to be expressly mentioned. Note the Lombard bands
and flat arches joining them.

103. BAYEUX   Towers

The Cathedral was burnt in 1107 by Henry I, and the church was rebuilt during the first
quarter of the century. To this period belong the western towers, and the lower part of the
nave appears to be a reconstruction after another fire in 1159. Early in the thirteenth
century all above the old arcades was pulled down and replaced by a lofty clerestory, and
a new vault was erected. The windows and buttresses shown here belong to this reconstruction, and at the same time the spires were placed on the western towers. This addition of
the spires necessitated a strengthening of the old towers; extra buttresses were provided,
and in places the actual walls, where pointed arches can be seen, were thickened.

104. Brantôme   Tower

Probably the oldest of a type common in South and West France, dating from the eleventh century. It stands apart from the church, and is composed of receding stages, the transition from one to the other in the upper part being masked by lofty gables. These gables are the first of a series which developed through such a fine tower as that at Saint-Léonard (pl. 109b) to transitional examples at Vendôme (pl. 110b) and Chartres (pl. 180), and to the graceful Gothic versions at Vernouillet and Senlis (pl. 193a).

105. (a) SAINT-RAMBERT   Tower   (b) MORIENVAL   Twin Towers

(a) A fine tower of the eleventh century. The straight-sided gables over the belfry windows are a variant on the tall gables which in one type of tower serve to mask the transition from one stage to the next (see that at Brantôme, pl. 104).

(b) Twin towers flank the apse, as at Tournai and many German churches. The north-eastern districts of France naturally had connexions with the Rhineland.

106. (a) ARLES   Saint-Trophime—tower   (b) ANZY-LE-DUC   Tower

(a) A twelfth-century tower retaining the flat Lombardic bands and arched cornices of the previous period. This conservative spirit is not uncommon in Provence, as also at Cruas (pl. 18), and in other places in the south, as at Saint-Aventin (pl. 95).

(b) In Burgundy and the Auvergne octagonal towers were favoured, especially over the crossing. This one, with its three similar stages and arched cornices, has a very Italian appearance, and would hardly look out of place in Lombardy itself.

107. (a) CUNAULT   Tower   (b) UZERCHE   Tower

(a) The tower at Cunault is placed in the south aisle, forming a kind of internal transept, and gets variety of effect by having a different number of windows to each stage. The lower stages, at any rate, are older than the rest of the church and may go back to the end of the eleventh century. The spire was added in the fifteenth.

(b) This is another example of the towers developed from the Brantôme type.

108. (a) POITIERS   (b) SAINT-JUNIEN   West tower
     Notre-Dame-la-Grande—tower

(a) The typical tower of the south-western school. A round top stage is placed on a square base, and is crowned with a low conical spire faced with a scale ornament, something like a stone edition of our Sussex shingles.

(b) In the Limousin and Loire Valley there are a number of churches with massive western porches carried up to form a tower. They are sometimes flanked by turrets, as here and at La Souterraine and Le Dorat. The most imposing of these tower-porches is the unfinished one at Saint-Benoît-sur-Loire (pl. 33), and there is another fine one at Ebreuil.

     The tower and façade date from the second half of the twelfth century. The middle part of the church dates from 1102 and contains the remarkable stone shrine of the saint, but there was an eastward extension *c.* 1230.

203   14-2

109. (a) DÉOLS   (b) SAINT-LÉONARD

109. (a) Déols   Tower

A fine specimen of square twelfth-century tower with spire. Spires being built of slightly overlapping or receding courses have no thrust, but where the transition from the square tower to the octagonal spire is abrupt an octagonal platform is produced by placing small arches across the corners, called squinches, and to prevent these from spreading they are weighted with pinnacles at the corners, a structural requirement thus producing one of the most effective ornamental features of later churches.

(b) Saint-Léonard   Tower

A late twelfth-century tower with open porch at the ground level, placed at the side instead of at the west end. The transition from the square to the octagonal upper stages of the pyramidal design is skilfully masked by the lofty gables of which we saw the embryo at Brantôme. Richard Cœur-de-Lion made a donation to the church in 1195, but exact dates of the work are not known. Damage by lightning necessitated repairs in the thirteenth and fifteenth centuries.

110.   (a) Auxerre   (b) Vendôme   Tower
Saint-Germain—west tower

Two examples showing the intermediate octagonal stage between the square tower and
spire. Both have the steep gables and corner pinnacles. In France, other than Normandy,
the pyramidal type with gradual transition from tower to spire, seems usually to have
been preferred to the type with well-marked division and corner pinnacles preferred in
England.

111. SAINT-GERMER   Apse and transept

There is no record of date, but it appears to be *c.* 1120–40. The apse with ambulatory and side-chapels is still quite Romanesque in appearance, although the internal construction is well on the way to Gothic (see p. 43). The original windows are all round-headed. In the thirteenth century (1259–72) the beautiful Lady Chapel, or Sainte-Chapelle, was added at the east end. (For the interior see pl. 195 b.)

112. Saint-Germer   Interior

This has been quoted (p. 43) as an early example of the Transitional style. Constructional arches are all pointed but the triforium arches and windows are still round-headed. There is a chevron, or zig-zag moulding round the arches of the sanctuary and on the ribs of the apse vault. The main vault is quadripartite, but those of the tribunes are still groined, and there are rudimentary flying buttresses above them which are kept below the outer roof.

113. LE MANS   Nave

Reconstructed after a fire in 1134, the present nave incorporates the aisles and one or two
arches of the old eleventh-century church, but the whole design was altered, the double-bay
system adopted with round columns and solid piers alternating, and a highly domed
cross-ribbed vault added over the centre. Traces of the old round arches can still be seen
outside the present arcade. The whole was consecrated in 1158. The magnificent choir was
rebuilt 1218–54 (see pl. 141).

114. PARIS   Saint-Denis—ambulatory of choir

This, and the westernmost bay of the nave and the west front, with the crypt, is the
surviving part of the church built by Abbot Suger, 1137–44. It has been much restored, and
it is possible that there may have been some reconstruction of the vaulting, when the
central part of the choir was rebuilt in the middle of the thirteenth century. If the vaulting
is actually Suger's work, it shows a remarkable mastery of the new Gothic manner of
erecting ribbed vaults round a curved ambulatory at this early date. The outer walls and
the slender pillars separating the two aisles are certainly the original work, but it is
difficult to see how the pillars of the main apse could have been renewed without recon-
structing the vaults.

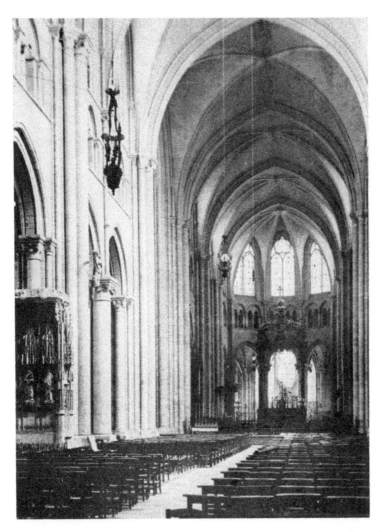

115. SENS CATHEDRAL   Interior

Probably the earliest of the great cathedrals in the Gothic style. In 1122 it was decided to
pull down the old basilica, in 1142 the work was in full swing, and in 1164 the High Altar
was consecrated by the Pope. The façade was still incomplete.

The alternate bay system, with twin columns between massive piers, and the sexpartite
vault were adopted. There was serious fire damage in 1184, and the vaults of the aisles seem
to have been reconstructed c. 1230. At the same time the clerestory windows were enlarged.

116. SENS   Ambulatory columns

The doubled columns are carried round the apse, and, alternately with solid piers, right through the nave. These double columns, the sexpartite vault and the French wide lancets were introduced by William of Sens in the new choir at Canterbury rebuilt under his supervision.

117. NOYON CATHEDRAL   Interior

One of the best examples of the earliest phase of Gothic. The church was burnt in 1131,
and the new choir was consecrated in 1157. The transepts seem to have been completed
c. 1170, and the western part of the nave c. 1180. We have the double bay system, roomy
tribunes, a shallow triforium above, making four stories in all. The vault was originally
sexpartite, but was rebuilt as quadripartite after a fire in 1293.
    This photograph was taken before the Great War, when very serious damage was done
by German bombardments. It has, however, been possible to restore the interior to
something approaching its original appearance, though considerable sections of the vault
had to be replaced and the walls still bear the marks of bullets and shell-fragments.

118. NOYON   Nave from aisle

Shows the roomy tribunes, and the simple early "crochet" capitals. There is a notable absence of mouldings round the arches, which look rather bare to English or Norman eyes.
    This also is a pre-War photograph.

119. NOYON   Interior of north transept

The transepts here are rounded, but without aisles. This feature is found at Tournai in Belgium, with which Noyon seems to have had close relations, and is common in the Rhineland. Several features in North-eastern France seem borrowed from German Romanesque, but are refined and treated in a thoroughly French manner. The pointed arch is used in the lowest and second stories, the round in the second and uppermost, showing a certain hesitation about rejecting the older form for decorative features.

215

120. LAON CATHEDRAL   Interior

Records of the building are not clear, but the church seems to have been begun *c.* 1160 and
finished apart from the towers *c.* 1205, when a fresh extension was undertaken, which
involved the pulling down of the apse and lengthening of the choir, which was given a
square east end, almost alone among the greater French churches (see pl. 149 a).

It has a sexpartite vault, but the extra shafts supporting the transverse arches are only
brought down to the massive capitals of the round columns, except in the eastern bays of
the nave, where extra shafts are added to four columns.

216

121. LAON   Nave from tribunes

This view from the tribunes shows the bay scheme, and four stories; also the roomy galleries of the tribunes, with the narrow triforium passage above. In the transepts, which no doubt were earlier than the nave, the round arch is still retained except in the main arcade.

122. REIMS   Saint-Rémi—exterior of apse

The choir of this ancient church was rebuilt 1170–90. For the interior see pl. 21. The grouping of triple lancet windows is characteristic of Champagne. The flying buttresses are good examples of the earliest type, after they had emerged from the aisle roofs, but before much attempt had been made to convert them into decorative features, or to weight them with pinnacles.

This is a pre-War photograph. Much damage was done to this fine church, but part of the choir-vault survived and it is possible something in the way of restoration may be attempted.

123. CHALONS-SUR-MARNE   Notre-Dame-en-Vaux—interior

The nave is based on an older one of *c.* 1145, but reconstructed and vaulted, probably after the completion of the choir. The latter was begun in 1157 and consecrated in 1183. The apse, with its tribunes, four stories and triple lancets in the clerestory, is very like that of Saint-Rémi at Reims.

124. CHALONS-SUR-MARNE   Notre-Dame—choir from transept

Shows the four stories, and richly-carved capitals. The tribunes are lighted by triple lancets. The aisle windows are, of course, fifteenth or early sixteenth-century insertions.

125. LISIEUX   Interior

Begun *c.* 1143, the nave and transepts were completed by 1181. The choir, in contrast to the usual practice, seems to have been left till last, but was finished in 1218. The apse, however, differs considerably in treatment and may be due to reconstruction after a fire which did some damage in 1226.

   The nave with its three stories and big round columns is in the style of the Ile-de-France, and bears considerable resemblance to Notre-Dame, Paris, except that the vault is quadripartite. This suggests that little progress was made in the first twenty years after 1143, for the style is much more that of *c.* 1170. The apse has richer mouldings and doubled columns and is more in the style of Normandy. The lantern tower is also a Norman feature.

126. LISIEUX   Columns of nave

The big round columns with massive capitals adorned with simple bold foliage have some resemblance to those of Paris. The vaulting shafts rest on the capitals. There is no alternation of heavy and lighter piers, such as would have been suitable for a sexpartite vault, which seems never to have been contemplated here.

127. SOISSONS   South transept

One of the most charming buildings of the late twelfth century, erected probably *c.* 1180. It was retained when the rest of the cathedral was rebuilt at the beginning of the thirteenth century. Like the transepts at Noyon it is apsidal, but has aisles, and a two-storied chapel opens out of it on the east side. There are four stories, and on the ground floor the sharp stilted arches, grouped in twos and threes with a beautiful string course of foliage above them, are particularly pleasing. The north transept is on the ordinary square plan.

(a)

(b)

128. Pontigny   (a) Exterior from south   (b) Exterior of apse

(a) The second of the four daughters of Citeaux, and the only one where much of the early church has survived. It is thus our most important example of a great Cistercian church. The original churches were very small, and the present building was begun *c.* 1150, and is thus a little later than Fontenay (see pl. 77) where more of the monastic buildings have survived. It is a good example of the extreme austerity of the Cistercian plan, with no towers or any ornament—merely a little bell-turret near the west end.

(b) The choir is an extension *c.* 1180–1200, when the square end usual in Cistercian churches was replaced by an apse with ambulatory in order to provide a series of chapels with extra altars at which each monk in priest's orders could officiate. All these chapels are included under a single roof, with none of the picturesque projections of the apsidal Romanesque chapels.

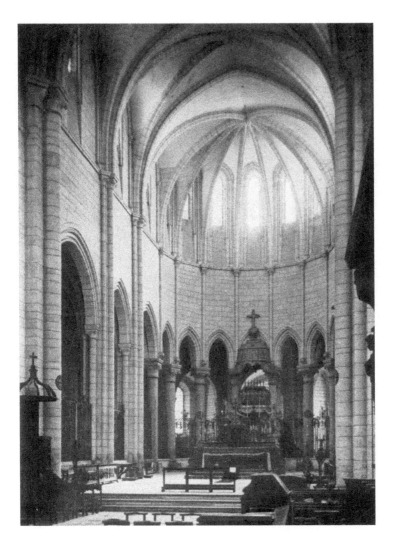

129. Pontigny   Interior of choir

A good example of early Burgundian Gothic, carried out in the simplest possible manner
to suit Cistercian taste. There are plain quadripartite vaults throughout, and no triforium,
blank walls being left to cover the space opposite the aisle roofs. The effect depends entirely
on proportions and suitability for its purpose. This is the part added *c.* 1180-1200.

225

130. AMIENS   Exterior from the quays

The outline of this, the crowning achievement of Ile-de-France Gothic, is strangely different from that
of a low English cathedral with its lofty towers, or even from those of Normandy like Coutances (see
pl. 150) or of earlier French churches like Laon. The vast roof, whose ridge is nearly 200 feet above
the ground, tends to dwarf the towers.

131. AMIENS   Exterior of apse

This was the last part of the main building to be completed apart from the nave chapels and upper parts of the west front. The choir was not begun till *c.* 1240, as it was desired to spare the old church of Saint-Firmin which occupied the ground, until the new nave was ready for occupation. The choir seems to have been finished in 1269, and shows a change in various details from the nave. The eastern chapels are so lofty as almost to dwarf the central apse, and their windows have advanced tracery in the heads with trefoils instead of circles. The flying buttresses are surmounted by a water channel supported by a light arcade (see p. 61) and this, with the over-elaborate balustrade, gives a sumptuous but rather fragile appearance to this part of the church.

227

132. AMIENS   Interior from west

The general effect as one enters this vast church by the west doors is overwhelming. The vault rises about 140 feet above the pavement, and the main piers are nearly twice the height of those of Notre-Dame, Paris. The Gothic scheme of a lofty vault supported mainly by buttresses is here carried to its extreme development, and as the main body of the church was completed in 50 years it is more homogeneous than most. The nave was begun in 1220 and finished c. 1236, after which the choir was taken in hand and the glass of the windows was placed in position in 1269. In the choir the main supports of the clerestory are brought down to form a single composition with the triforium, and as the outer wall of the latter is glazed, a light and brilliant effect is produced. Little gables over the triforium arcade are rather meaningless but add to the richness of the work.

133. AMIENS   Nave from south transept

This gives some idea of the magnificent scale of the main arcade. Even the bombastic
vulgarity of the eighteenth-century pulpit and altar-piece is rendered insignificant by the
vast scale of the building. There is a beautiful string-course of foliage below the triforium.

134. AMIENS   North transept looking into nave

Here again the great height is shown, and the design of the nave-bays is clearly seen. The
big clerestory windows fill the whole space between the buttresses and the vault. There are
some richly carved early sixteenth-century screens in the transepts as well as on the choir
enclosures. The woodwork of the stalls also dates from the same period and is the finest
example of its kind in existence. It excited Ruskin's unbounded enthusiasm.

135. BEAUVAIS   From tower of Saint-Étienne

This view of this vast fragment of a church towering above the roofs gives some idea of the immensity
of its scale. Begun in 1225, five years after Amiens, it was intended to surpass all other cathedrals, but
this ambition met with disaster as some of the buttresses gave way in 1284 and part of the vault collapsed.
Reconstruction of the choir was not completed till *c.* 1322, after which the work languished till *c.* 1500.
During the first half of the sixteenth century the transepts and one bay of the nave were erected, and in
1569 a lantern tower was begun 500 feet high, which collapsed in 1573. In two years the damage was
patched up, but all attempts to rebuild the tower were abandoned as dangerous, and funds were
lacking to build the nave. The old Carolingian nave, called the Basse-Œuvre, was therefore spared, and
its three windows and roof can be seen in our picture and serve to emphasis the colossal scale of the
new cathedral.

136. Beauvais   Interior

The shortness of this half-church in relation to its height makes it difficult to obtain a really worthy photograph. The vault is 157 feet above the pavement, and surpasses all others. The clerestory windows, nearly 60 feet high, are combined with the glazed triforium in one composition as at Amiens. There are double aisles, the inner having its own triforium and clerestory. The pillars on the extreme left with smooth double-curve section are part of the sixteenth-century rebuilding after the fall of the tower, and contrast with the shafts and hollows of the thirteenth-century pier opposite.

137. BEAUVAIS   South side of choir

This shows the way in which repairs were effected after the disaster of 1284. An extra pier
was built between each of the others, and two sharply-pointed arches built inside each
of the original wide ones, traces of which can still be made out in the wall. Although
something of a makeshift, this narrowing of the bays and multiplication of parts adds to the
apparent size, and no other building gives such an impression of height and magnificence.

138. CHARTRES   Interior

(From a photograph by the late S. Gardner)

With the exception of the lower part of the west front which survived owing to protection by the solid towers, the cathedral was rebuilt after the fire of 1194. It is on a magnificent scale and very solidly built. The greater part seems to have been finished by 1220, and the wonderful porches of the transepts were added between that date and 1250. The height of the vault is about 122 feet, and of the windows of the apse about 46 feet. In the eighteenth century the lower part of the choir was embellished with marble and stucco in the deplorable taste of the period.

235   16-2

139. CHARTRES   Nave from transept

This shows the main features of the bay design. Chartres is famous for its thirteenth-century glass which is accounted the finest in existence. There is also some very beautiful twelfth-century glass in the west windows. It is also exceptionally rich in sculpture, of the twelfth century in the west porches, of the thirteenth in the transept porches (see pls. 186, 187), and of the early sixteenth in the screen round the choir.

40. LE MANS   Exterior from the east

A new choir on a vast scale was added to the old cathedral between 1218 and 1254. The planning of its double aisles, ambulatory and chapels with their vaults and buttresses are considered by many authorities to have been the most satisfactory solution of the problems ever achieved. The transepts and tower were added in the fifteenth century, but the nave dating from the eleventh and twelfth centuries remains (see pl. 113).

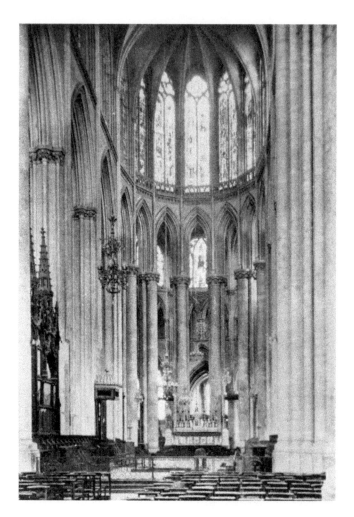

141. Le Mans   Interior of choir

This splendid thirteenth-century choir, some 112 feet high to the vault, contrasts strongly with the older nave, which is about 78½ feet high. There is actually a large window looking westward above the nave roof. The inner aisles of the choir have their three stories, and the triforium has much beautiful foliage carving, but the choir itself is only of two stories, without a triforium. This arrangement with lofty arches on twin-columns round the apse is very like that at Coutances (see pl. 151), and the richness of the mouldings also resembles the treatment in the neighbouring province of Normandy.

142. LE MANS   Interior of ambulatory

This shows the arrangement of the aisles and chapels round the apse. The inner aisle has
its three stories, and the outer only one. This again shows the rich mouldings and the
round abacus above the capitals, which is commoner in Normandy and England than
elsewhere in France. The capital in the centre is an example of the crocket capital ("à
crochet") formed of stiff stalks turned over in a tight little bunch of leaves, which is a
favourite French convention.

143. ROUEN CATHEDRAL   South aisle of nave

Begun after the fire of 1200, the story of the building is somewhat obscure. There was a
change in design during construction as the aisle-vault was abolished and the vault of the
tribunes made to serve in its place. The arches leading into it, however, were retained and
a passage managed by corbelling out a little platform supported by slender shafts over the
piers in the aisle. There are thus four stories, in spite of the abolition of the tribune galleries.
The clerestory windows were enlarged later.

Rouen, being of a more moderate height—92 feet—has a fine lantern tower crowned by
a monstrous iron spire, and with its wealth of mouldings seems more homely to English
eyes than the greater cathedrals. The transept fronts were not finished till 1278, and the
west front and the great Tour de Beurre were not completed till the beginning of the
sixteenth century.

144. REIMS   Interior

This photograph, taken before the War, shows an unusual effect of lighting, as the clerestory
windows retained their fine thirteenth-century glass, while that of the aisles had been
destroyed. The plan is simple, with a triforium of four plain arches, and vaulting shafts
reaching the ground. The whole was very solidly built—much more so than Amiens—
or it would not have been possible to restore it after the War. Huge gaps were made in the
vault, buttresses were smashed, and much damage was done by the fire which destroyed
the outer roof, but fortunately some of the glass was removed to safety and has been replaced.
The nave has been made available for services for some time, but the restoration of the
choir is only now (1937) approaching completion.

The vault, which is about 125 feet high, is more sharply pointed than those of Amiens
or Beauvais.

The rebuilding after the fire of 1210 was begun in 1211, and the choir was finished in
1241. The western half of the nave is later than the eastern, and must be assigned to the
master-mason Bernard de Soissons, who made the rose window, and was in charge of the
work from 1255 to 1290.

145. REIMS   Nave from south transept

This photograph was also taken before the War. The naturalistic carving of the capitals in
the eastern part of the nave, erected before 1250, is very beautiful (see pl. 200 a), but that
of the later western bays is more crowded and confused, anticipating fourteenth-century
style. Bands of foliage are carried round the subsidiary shafts to bring the capitals to the
same size as those of the main central column, instead of keeping them proportionate to the
size of the shafts, as at Chartres, Amiens and most other places.

146. BOURGES   Exterior, south side

The exact dates of Bourges are not known, but it seems to have been begun *c.* 1200, or possibly a few years earlier. The choir was finished *c.* 1220, and the nave probably *c.* 1250–60. It is planned as a vast hall without any division or transept. This picture shows the flying buttresses and plate-tracery of the clerestory windows. In the fifteenth century chapels were built between the buttresses, and the north tower was built after the collapse of the original one in 1506.

147. BOURGES   Exterior of apse

This is almost a continuation of the last plate, but a few bays would have been omitted.
The double aisles with flying buttresses covering them in two stages, with a central support
resting on the piers between them, can be clearly seen. The whole view of the cathedral
from the south is most impressive.

148. Bourges   Interior

The general view of the interior from the west is overwhelming. The double aisles, with chapels outside them, are carried right round the building, and the great breadth, the forest of columns and lofty central vault about 125 feet high combine to make a marvellous whole. The sexpartite vault and consequent alternation of rather heavier and lighter piers are early features. The immense height of the piers, some 55 feet, combined with a certain poverty of mouldings, produces rather a wire-drawn effect, and tends to give the upper stories a depressed appearance, but this is compensated by the three stories of the inner aisles, which are very lofty and narrow, and by the splendour of the glass, which is almost a rival for that of Chartres.

149. (a) LAON   East end   (b) BAYEUX   East end

(a) Laon is almost unique among the great churches of France in having a square east end. It resulted from an extension made soon after completion of the twelfth-century church, and the nature of the ground or existing buildings seem to have made this form necessary. The square end, though unusual, is less rare in smaller churches.

(b) Bayeux has the usual curved chevet with ambulatory and chapels, but the latter, though polygonal inside, are enclosed by a simple curved arcade outside, an elaboration of the early Cistercian plan at Pontigny (see pl. 128b).

The central lantern tower is fifteenth-century work, but the dome and upper part were rebuilt on a new design in the nineteenth century.

150. COUTANCES   Exterior from the east

Being of moderate size, with a vault about 92 feet high, the lofty towers, spires and pinnacles give Coutances an outline which compares very favourably with Amiens (see pl. 130). The great lantern tower over the crossing, even though it lacks its spire, is the finest thing of its kind in France. The dates are not accurately known, but the whole church appears to be work of the first half of the thirteenth century, with few later additions.

The flying buttresses have a very wide spread to cover the double aisles round the apse, and rest on the walls between the outer chapels.

151. Coutances   Interior of choir

This very pleasing design is probably the prototype of its greater rival, the choir of Le Mans. It has double aisles, the inner one with three stories, but the lofty arches of the main arcade correspond to the three divisions of the adjoining aisle. There is no triforium, merely a little balustrade and platform below the clerestory windows. Round the apse the columns are coupled, and we have the rich mouldings of Normandy. The ridge-rib at the crown of the vault is an English feature.

152.　COUTANCES   Aisles of the ambulatory

The double aisles with shallow chapels beyond produce pleasing vistas. The ingenious
schemes for arranging the ribs of the vault to cover the curved space would have been
impossible before the invention of the pointed arch with its variable curves. Note also the
crocket capitals with the round abacus of Normandy and England, and the water-holding
mouldings of the bases, with which we are familiar in England as a good guide to a date in
the earlier thirteenth century.

153. COUTANCES   Upper stories of north transept

The deep hollows of the tower-arch mouldings and the tall lancet window at the end are again instances of the resemblance of style in England and Normandy, both, no doubt, derived from a common Romanesque original, but separating as French influence affected the plans and other features. The numerous wall-passages for inspection and repairs are also a Normandy speciality.

154. CAEN   Saint-Étienne (Abbaye aux Hommes)—choir

This fine early Gothic choir was added to the Conqueror's Church *c.* 1200, but there do not seem to be any exact records. The bay scheme of the Romanesque nave with its roomy tribunes is continued, but the vaulting is quadripartite, and the graceful Gothic forms are in strong contrast with the severe arches of the eleventh-century nave.

155. CAEN   Saint-Étienne—choir

This shows the early Gothic version of the Romanesque tribunes, lighted from the back by circular windows. The clerestory windows are very short, as the vault of the tribunes has to be protected by a lean-to roof, and there is here no extra triforium, as at Laon.

The star-shaped piercings in the spandrels of the main arcade, the clustered shafts and multiplicity of mouldings are all characteristic of Normandy. The cable ornament in the central moulding of the arches is reminiscent of Romanesque, or Norman as we should call it in England.

156. CAEN   Saint-Étienne—ambulatory

Here, again, we find resemblances to work in England, especially in the work done under French influence at Canterbury. The diagonal vault ribs appear to be nearly round, and the pointed transverse ribs are decorated with zig-zag mouldings. The clustered shafts and round abacus above the capitals are good examples of the methods used in Normandy.

157. ROUEN CATHEDRAL   Columns of sanctuary from Lady Chapel

The vista looking west from the early fourteenth-century Lady Chapel is striking. The cylindrical columns of the choir, with round Normandy abacus, contrast with the many-shafted piers of the nave which are so like English work. The capitals are of the crocket type, and the light thrown by the lantern tower over the crossing can be seen in this photograph. The date of the choir is not recorded, but seems to be early thirteenth century, part of the rebuilding after the fire of 1200.

255

158. BRAISNE   Abbey Church of Saint-Yved

Said to have been consecrated in 1216, and a good example of the early Gothic of Champagne. There is no ambulatory, and the shafts of the quadripartite vaulting are brought to the ground, or rest on the large capitals of cylindrical columns. The plain four-arched triforium (two-arched round the apse) is very like that at Reims, but the plain wide lancet windows look a little earlier than those of the great cathedral, while the general style is perhaps nearer to that of Laon. The church was probably begun in the latter part of the twelfth century. It has lost its western bays, but possesses some fragments of what must have been some particularly fine sculpture.

256

159. Vézelay   Ambulatory of choir

The choir of this famous abbey was rebuilt towards the end of the twelfth century in the
new Gothic style. Some features of transitional character are retained, such as the round
arch in the triforium and windows of the chapels, and a rather experimental arrangement
of the vaulting in the bay next the apse, where a half-bay is introduced resting on much
more slender columns than the rest. On the walls between the chapels rows of columns
of a purely decorative nature are introduced without any architectural function.

160. AUXERRE   Choir aisle and ambulatory

Auxerre is a delightful town full of archaeological interest, and the view from the banks of
the Yonne of the town and its four great churches is one of the most striking in France (see
Frontispiece).

The choir was built 1215–34 and is a beautiful specimen of pure Gothic, with its beauty
much enhanced by the preservation of a great part of its thirteenth-century glass. The
curve of the ambulatory is not interrupted by chapels, as only the Lady Chapel at the
east was built. The foliage of the capitals is beautiful naturalistic work (see pl. 200 b).

161. Auxerre   Lady Chapel

An exceedingly graceful construction of the first quarter of the thirteenth century. The tall
and very slender columns of fine stone from Tonnerre have shown no signs of weakness
although a considerable amount of weight is thrown upon them. They were introduced
to solve the problem of how to carry the ribs of the circular ambulatory across the wide
opening to the Lady Chapel.

162. PARIS   Saint-Denis—interior

Suger's church having fallen into disrepair, it was decided to rebuild it less than 100 years after its erection. The new building was begun in 1231 and was completed *c.* 1267. The master-mason was Pierre de Montereau, who preserved the ambulatory and eastern chapels and the west front, but rebuilt the body of the church on the most up-to-date lines. The full Gothic scheme was developed to the fullest extent, with rigid economy of material, logical and scientific balance of thrusts and the whole space between the buttresses occupied by windows. It was one of the first instances where the triforium was glazed, and windows were filled with magnificent glass, much of which has unfortunately perished.

163. CHALONS-SUR-MARNE   Cathedral—nave arcade

Begun in 1248 this imposing church was mostly built during the second half of the thirteenth century, and is a good example of fully developed Gothic. The lofty arcade on the tall cylindrical columns and the large Geometric windows, many of them containing fine glass, make up a noble whole in spite of seventeenth-century mutilations in the apse and a pompous Classical façade.

164. Sées   Exterior from the south

The only record of date is the death in 1292 of the bishop who was described as the builder of the cathedral. The style is fairly advanced, and obviously not earlier than the middle of the century, while the choir and possibly the openwork spires may not have been finished till well on into the fourteenth. The lightness of construction was pushed to excess, and as insufficient care was devoted to the foundations very large sums have had to be spent at various times on restoration and upkeep.

165. Sées   Interior of choir

The choir of late thirteenth or early fourteenth-century work is very graceful and pretty
if it misses the grandeur of the greater cathedrals. Crocketed gables are placed over the
main arches, exaggerations of those in the triforium of the choir at Amiens, and the
Normandy love of ornament and mouldings is much in evidence. The triforium is merely
a prolongation of the clerestory, but with double tracery to allow of a narrow passage, and
as the outer windows are glazed and the aisle-windows are very large, the church is
brilliantly lit.

263

166. MEAUX   Interior of choir

The history of this cathedral presents an archaeological puzzle owing to the way in which it has been reconstructed and restored at various times. The original church seems to have been begun before 1198, but fell into disrepair and had to be reconstructed early in the fourteenth century. The straight bays of the choir have what may be described as false tribunes with arches opening into the aisles like those at Rouen (see pl. 143). It is said that a real gallery never existed here, but that this arrangement was adopted to correspond with the nave where there were originally four stories, but where the tribunes were subsequently abolished to provide loftier arcades.

167. TROYES CATHEDRAL   Interior of choir

The choir was begun in 1208 and finished 1223, but was severely damaged by a storm in
1227 and the repairs seem to have been carried out very slowly. The present appearance
is of the second half of the thirteenth century, and the lightness of the construction with
the stone supports reduced to a minimum, the whole of the space between filled with
windows, and a glazed triforium, make this a veritable lantern of glass. In spite of a great
amount of restoration of the stonework and patching of the glass, the effect of such a mass
of gorgeous thirteenth-century mosaic glass is overwhelmingly magnificent. In some ways
it is even more striking than Chartres itself, as, although the quality of the glass may not
quite equal that of its western rival, the mass of it with so little stone to interrupt the blaze
of jewel-like colour is extraordinarily fine.

168. TROYES CATHEDRAL   Choir from aisle

This again shows the immense amount of space occupied by the clerestory windows and
the glazed triforium which continues them. They are good specimens of the "Rayonnant"
or Geometric type of tracery, but the general tendency of such windows in France is to
make the mullions and tracery bars much smaller than those used in England, though the
earliest ones at Reims are heavier. In this light tracery more reliance was placed on the
iron bars supporting the glass than was usual in England.

169. Troyes   Saint-Urbain—exterior

This church is usually quoted as the extreme example of economy of material and walls of glass. Thanks to the quality of the stone available, it has been treated almost like metal. If the documentary evidence were not so full, we should have hesitated to class this as a thirteenth-century church owing to its advanced style, but it is known that it was begun in 1262 and that the bulk of it was completed by about 1276. The western portion of the nave has never been finished, and that end has been patched up in more recent times.

170. TROYES   Saint-Urbain—interior

There is no ambulatory, and the apse is apparently almost entirely of glass. The windows
are so large that they are filled by bands of brilliantly coloured figure subjects set in plain
light patterns, called grisaille. The tracery is of the "Rayonnant" type.

171. ANGERS CATHEDRAL   Interior

Shows the Angevin type of vault described on p. 55. There are no aisles or pillars, and the
plan is that of the Romanesque domed churches. Heavy transverse ribs divide the nave
into squares, which are covered by a ribbed vault rising to a point 9 or 10 feet above the
transverse arches.

   Fine tapestries hide the wall arcade with a shallow platform below the windows, but
a monstrosity of a baldachino detracts from the dignity of a fine simple design. The church
was begun c. 1150 and was built on the foundations of an older church, whose arcades were
abolished.

172. Poitiers Cathedral   Interior

Another rather later example of the Angevin style. As is not infrequent in the south-west,
nave and aisles are practically the same height, enabling the necessary lighting to be
obtained from lofty windows in the aisles.

The vaulting is highly domical, with very slight ribs, including one starting from the
apex of the transverse arches.

It was begun by Henry II of England in 1162, and is said to have been almost completed
with the exception of the façade before his death in 1189.

173. Bayeux Cathedral   Interior of choir

A fine example of the rich Gothic of Normandy. Note the elaborate mouldings of the triforium, and the rosettes and spandrel carvings. The proportions, too, are more those to which we are accustomed in England.

A consecration took place in 1231, but as the style looks fairly advanced it is possible that the church was not completed before the middle of the century. The fluting of the round pillars of the apse is an affectation of the eighteenth century, fortunately not carried further.

174. BAYEUX   Ambulatory and chapels

Very elegant work, which again is difficult to date before the middle of the thirteenth century. Note the double tracery of the windows. There appears to have been a certain amount of restoration, especially in the wall arcades.

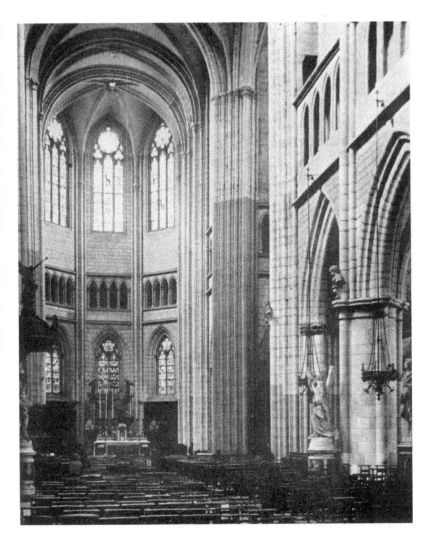

175. Dijon   Saint-Benigne—interior

This church replaces the famous old basilica of *c.* 1000, of which part only of the crypt remains. The present church dates from *c.* 1280, and is an example of Burgundian Gothic. The apse has no ambulatory or chapels, and details are mostly simple.

176. (a) CHARTRES   Nave buttresses   (b) BEAUVAIS   Apse buttresses

(a) The Chartres buttresses are magnificently solid, and the impression of strength is enhanced by the heavy round arch joining them at the top and enclosing the windows, shown in pl. 178 a.

(b) Those at Beauvais show the wonderful scaffolding of stone required to support the lofty vault. This photograph is taken from the aisle-roof.

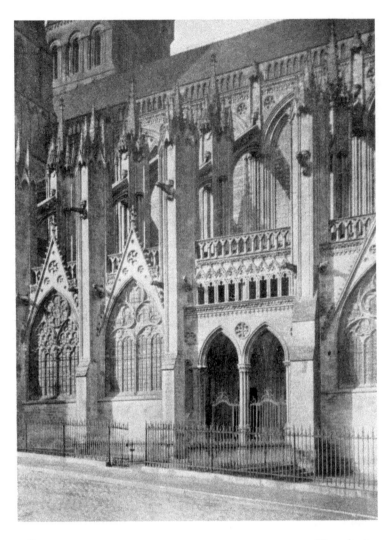

177. BAYEUX   Nave buttresses

This fine range of flying buttresses was built when the thirteenth-century clerestory and
vault were placed above the old Romanesque nave. Later on, as was often the case, chapels
were added between the buttresses. The tracery of the window next the porch is a good
example of Flamboyant style.

(a)

(b)

178. (a) CHARTRES   (b) REIMS

178. (a) Chartres   Clerestory windows

These show the first stage in the development from plain lancets towards plate tracery.
Two lancets are grouped together and a circle placed above them. The cusping is merely
provided by the iron bars supporting the glass.

(b) Reims   Buttresses

The heavy pinnacles, whose function it is to direct the outward thrust from the vaults
downwards, have become a decorative feature, and the great angels with outspread wings
in the niches produce a magnificent effect.

The tracery in the window of the tower flanking the transept marks an early stage in
the development of bar-tracery, the spandrels between circle and lancets being pierced,
and the form of the stone-tracery has become as important as the shape of the openings.

179. Rose Windows
    (a) Chartres   West front   (b) Chalons-sur-Marne   Transept

These show the contrast between the plate-tracery at Chartres at the beginning of the thirteenth century and the more elaborate scheme at Chalons at the end of the century. In the latter the rose is combined with the triforium stage to form a single composition, and the intervening spaces are opened out and filled with glass so as to occupy the whole space between the enclosing framework of the transept end with one vast window.

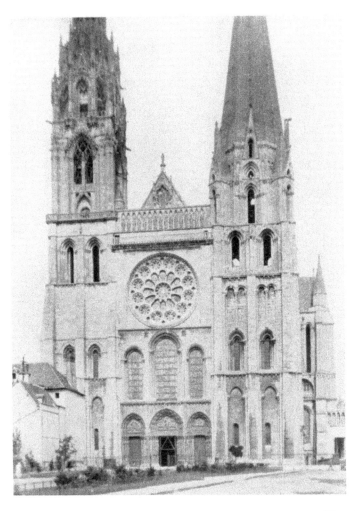

180. CHARTRES   West front

The north tower is the older, up to roof-level, and the south including the spire followed soon after, both dating from the middle of the twelfth century. The south tower is the finest example of its type, showing the gradual conversion from the square to the octagon, masked by gables, as contrasted with the English and Normandy type with a well-marked division between tower and spire. The porch was originally placed at the inner side of the towers but was subsequently rebuilt flush with the outer sides. The rose window (see pl. 179 a) belongs to the rebuilding of the nave on a vast scale at the beginning of the thirteenth century. The great height of the newer church tends to spoil the proportions of the grand southern steeple. The elaborate upper part of the north tower with its richly-carved spire was added early in the sixteenth century.

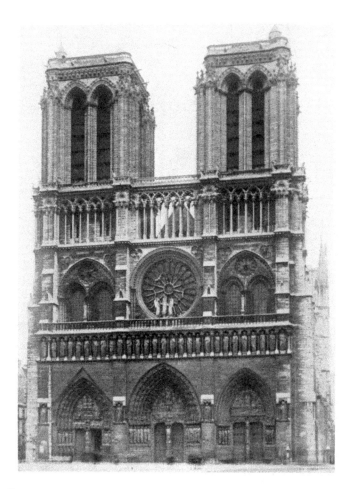

181. PARIS   Notre-Dame—west front

The strong horizontal lines are a distinguishing feature of this noble composition. The
three porches full of sculptures, the gallery of kings above, the rose window and open
arcading joining the twin towers are the regular components of the typical French façade.
    The cathedral was begun in 1163, but only some of the sculptures of the southern doorway
belong to that period. The actual building of the façade did not begin till the thirteenth
century, and the three doorways were standing by 1208. It was ready up to the open
gallery in 1220, but the towers were not finished till the middle of the century. The large
statues and the popular gargoyles of the upper gallery were made under Viollet-le-Duc,
who was responsible for the restoration after the damage wrought at the Revolution. The
sculpture of the tympana over the doors, with the exception of the lower part of the central
one, is original and very fine. Though the solid buttresses of the towers seem to suggest an
intention to crown them with spires, these were never erected.

182. Laon   Façade and towers

The cathedral was begun *c.* 1160 at the east end (this part subsequently remodelled), and the west front and its towers were finished during the first quarter of the thirteenth century. It consists of the same elements as Paris, but the horizontal lines are less emphasized. There has been a good deal of restoration, especially in the lower part. The towers with their open-work buttresses were famous, even in the Middle Ages, when Villard de Honnecourt, a thirteenth-century master-mason, made drawings of them in his sketch-book, which has survived. The statues of oxen at the corners of the upper stages are said to commemorate the beasts who hauled the stones up the hill to build the cathedral.

183. Coutances   West front

These spires form with the lantern tower over the crossing one of the grandest groups in France, though the large staircase turrets on the outside produce a slightly lop-sided effect from some aspects. The exact dates of Coutances do not seem to be recorded, but we may safely regard the façade as mid-thirteenth-century work. The gallery between the towers is later. The rose window is replaced by a large window of the ordinary shape, as is usual in Normandy.

184. AMIENS   West front

Begun in 1220, the façade up to the bottom of the rose window was completed by 1236,
after which there seems to have been an interruption. Work on the south tower was resumed
in 1366, but the north tower and the gallery between the two only date from the beginning
of the fifteenth century.

The three great cavernous porches filled with superb sculpture and placed between the
boldly projecting buttresses make up a magnificent composition, and the whole effect of
this mighty cliff of carved stone rising over 220 feet above the ground is overwhelmingly
grand.

185. Reims   West front

Carried out more according to one consistent design than Amiens, this façade is more harmonious though perhaps lacking some of the rugged strength of its rival. It was begun about the middle of the thirteenth century, and the rose was opened before 1290. The upper parts of the towers were not completed for some time after. The two little gables on the outer buttresses give almost the effect of the five porches of Bourges. The sculpture, though of varying quality and by different hands, reaches the high-water mark of Gothic art.

This photograph, taken since the War, shows how far the restorers have been able to repair the damage done by German shells. The buttresses of the north tower have been allowed to retain some traces of their wounds, but the rest has been very skilfully restored.

186. CHARTRES   North porc

The transept porches at Chartres are even more elaborate than the earlier western porch. They are eac
said to contain over 700 figures, large and small, and the sculpture is of supreme interest both from
the artistic and iconographical points of view. The inner doorways were first put in hand and mu
have been completed during the first 20 years of the thirteenth century, but the outer piers and gable
seem to have been added later, about the middle of the century.

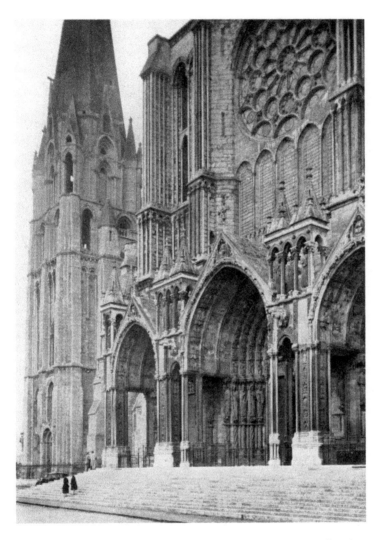

187. CHARTRES   South porch

As with the north porch the inner doorways were first taken in hand and the outer porch
added *c*. 1250. There are a series of small reliefs instead of statues on the outer piers.
The fine south-west tower is well seen in the background (see under pl. 180).

188. CHARTRES   South porch

Another view of the porch shown in pl. 187. These transepts are flanked by low towers,
like a western façade, but in this case the towers were not carried up to any great height.

189. AMIENS   West porches

These vast cavernous porches with their wealth of sculpture are in strong contrast with the
English scheme as represented at Wells or Salisbury, where the idea is to preface the
cathedral with a great screen, like a colossal reredos, in which the doors are made small
so as not to interfere with the design, and variety of surface depends upon the bold projecting
buttresses.

Date 1220–40.

190. BOURGES   West porches

The five porches, ranged across the great breadth of the double-aisled church, provide the most imposing entry to any cathedral. The big statues have perished, but the reliefs in the tympana, especially the great "Doom" over the central door, are of great interest.

The two doorways on the south side appear to be *c.* 1250–60, and the central *c.* 1275. The two on the north were only rebuilt after the fall of the north tower in 1506, and were finished *c.* 1515.

290

191. Auxerre   West front, south door

This very elegant doorway is an excellent example of the delicate work of the second half of the thirteenth century. The large statues, which were no longer column figures, but stood in niches, have perished, but the rest of the sculpture is exquisitely graceful. The large relief beside the porch represents the Judgment of Solomon.

192. REIMS   Statues of western porc

Although sculpture cannot be included in this volume, this group of magnificent statues, marking
high-water mark of Gothic art, may be introduced in order to illustrate the method of decorating the ja
of the deeply recessed porches with large figures set against the columns supporting the canopies. In
early work of *c.* 1150–70 at Chartres the statues are abnormally tall and thin, corresponding to the shaft
which they are attached and thus fulfil their architectural function admirably. At Reims natural proporti
have been attained, and the figures are less constrained and almost free from their architectural surroundi
though quiet attitudes and stately simplicity keep them still in harmony with the lines of the building.

This photograph was taken before the War. Those on the left were very badly damaged or destroyed,
the group of the Presentation in the Temple on the right escaped with minor injuries.

193. (a) SENLIS   Spire   (b) CAEN   Saint-Pierre—spire

Two of the finest examples of the rival types favoured in the Ile-de-France and Normandy respectively.

At Senlis the famous spire was erected on the late twelfth-century tower *c.* 1240. It is built on the pyramidal plan, with no sharp distinction between tower and spire, the transition being made by an octagonal section the corners of which are marked by pinnacles, turrets and sharp gables, whose remote ancestors appeared at Brantôme (see pl. 104).

The spire at Caen built in 1308 is perhaps the finest example of the Normandy type, with well-marked division between tower and spire, elaborate parapet and open-work pinnacles at the junction. The very lofty belfry lights are also characteristic of the province.

194. (a) LAON   (b) SAINT-PÈRE-SOUS-VÉZELAY
    South transeptal tower   Tower

(a) One of the group of five towers, which give Laon Cathedral such a striking outline (compare pl. 182 for the western towers). The two towers on the east side of the transepts were never completed. The spires no longer exist. This tower was built a few years after the western pair *c.* 1230.

(b) This fine tower was built *c.* 1240, and seems to have been inspired by those at Laon. The wooden spire is not ancient.

195. (a) COUTANCES
    Interior of central lantern tower

(b) SAINT-GERMER
    Interior of Sainte-Chapelle

a) A beautiful example of mid-thirteenth-century detail, with the sharply pointed arches, deep mouldings and conventional foliage of Normandy. The bold foliage cornice approaches the English stiff-leaf convention, though it is not quite the same.

b) Built between 1259 and 1272 this lovely little chapel is typical of the fully developed later Gothic (or "Rayonnant") ideal. Wall spaces are almost entirely eliminated and all the detail is masterly. Much fine thirteenth-century glass remains, and the building may be compared with the slightly earlier Sainte-Chapelle in Paris, though the latter has suffered much from over-restoration.

(a) (b) (c)

196. (a) TOULOUSE   Saint-Sernin—central steeple
     (b) LES SAINTES MARIES DE LA MER   Fortified church
     (c) LIMOGES CATHEDRAL   Tower

(a) Typical of the characteristic brick architecture developed in Toulouse. The three lower round-arched stages are *c.* 1130–40, the next two *c.* 1260–70, and the spire fifteenth-century (somewhat restored). Other examples of this brick style may be found in Toulouse and at Saint-Lizier, etc.

(b) In its exposed position by the sea, liable to raids by pirates, this church was built to look more like a castle than a sacred edifice. Conditions in Southern France were very unsettled, especially in the fourteenth century, and fortified churches are not uncommon. Well-known examples may be cited at Saint-Victor, Marseilles; the church of the Knights of St John of Jerusalem at Luz; the great cathedral at Albi (see pl. 206), and the old cathedral at Agde.

(c) Limoges developed a local type of tower, in which the octagon is so placed on the square that the angles come in the middle of the face. There is another example at Saint-Michel-aux-Lions at Limoges that has preserved the spire, which the tower of the cathedral has lost.

197. ROUEN CATHEDRAL   Detail of west doors

A rich example of the conventional foliage of the first quarter of the thirteenth century.

(a)

(b)

(c)

198. Examples of Twelfth-century Foliage

198. Examples of Twelfth-century Foliage
    (a) Reims   Saint-Rémi—western bays
    (b) Chalons-sur-Marne   Notre-Dame
    (c) Laon Cathedral

(a) Built *c.* 1170–90 and retaining much Classical feeling treated freely, but based on the acanthus.

(b) A curious survival of early interlacements. Probably part of the older nave of *c.* 1145, incorporated in the reconstructed nave of *c.* 1180.

(c) *c.* 1180, a mixture of figure and foliage.

(a)

(b)

199. THIRTEENTH-CENTURY FOLIAGE
   (a) BAYEUX   Doorway in interior of nave
   (b) CHARTRES   North porch

(a) A fine scroll of semi-naturalistic type favoured in Normandy.
(b) Naturalistic foliage of *c.* 1220–40.

(a)

(b)

200. THIRTEENTH-CENTURY FOLIAGE
  (a) REIMS   Capital in nave
  (b) AUXERRE   Capital of choir

(a) Mid-thirteenth century. The famous "Vintage" capital mixed with figures. The leaves of naturalistic type are arranged with some formality but much freedom. Later work in the nave, *c.* 1280, shows them as though plucked and stuck on without much feeling for composition.

(b) Naturalistic work *c.* 1230.

201. SOISSONS   Saint-Jean des Vignes—cloister

Although much ruined and broken, this cloister remains an excellent example of the rich
work of the second half of the thirteenth century.

2. TROYES   Nave from aisles

Troyes Cathedral was a very long time building. The lower part of the nave was begun in the fourteenth century, but the high vault was only finished in 1497. The general character is, however, of the earlier date. The graceful triforium with back wall glazed, the large clerestory windows, the vaulting shafts carried down to the ground without interruption, are all characteristic of the logical scheme of the second phase of Gothic. Broad in proportion to the height of the vault—some 95 feet—with double aisles, the effect is one of spaciousness, a forest of piers lit by a superb series of windows, thirteenth-century in the choir and later in the nave.

203. AUXERRE CATHEDRAL   Nave

Begun *c.* 1334, but not completed till the following century. A logical if somewhat cold
design, with vaulting shafts running down to the ground without a break, and capitals of
the arcade reduced to insignificance. The chief decorative feature consists in the enormous
clerestory windows, which provide a wide field for the coloured glass.

304

204. NEVERS CATHEDRAL   Interior

The nave, to which the nearest bays belong, is a thirteenth-century work, whose most remarkable feature is the introduction of little figures playing round the bases of the triforium shafts. The choir is a good example of fourteenth-century style. It is comparatively low, and in the apse the triforium is practically thrown into the clerestory; clustered shafts with small capitals and shallower mouldings contrast with the bolder work of the earlier nave, but the change is more one of detail than of general design.

205. RAMPILLON   West doorway

Built at the very end of the thirteenth century this doorway is a good example of the change
then coming in from the regular thirteenth-century plan. The statues are no longer column
figures, but each is set in a separate niche, and although the figures are natural and capable
productions they suffer some loss of dignity and architectural feeling in consequence. The
Christ of the trumeau is the best of them and a particularly pleasing figure, and the little
"Doom" reliefs of the lintel are graceful though treated in a less monumental style than the
earlier versions of the subject.

Rampillon (near Provins) was a church belonging to the Knights of St John of Jerusalem.

206. ALBI CATHEDRAL   From the east

This extraordinary fortress church was begun in 1282 and finished *c.* 1390. It is of red brick, and the plain walls, divided by rounded tower-like buttresses, rise to a height of over 130 feet. Narrow slits of windows at a considerable distance from the ground and a great castle tower at the west end complete the fortress appearance. The parapet is a restoration; at one time it was proposed to place little turrets all round, but the effect was not liked and only one retained.

207. ALBI   Interior

The vast interior has a vault-span of 62 feet, and, as described on p. 69, the buttresses are brought inside, and two stories of chapels introduced between them. The vault is 98½ feet high, and it and the walls are covered with sixteenth-century frescoes of Italian style.

The extremely rich screen which enclosed the ritual choir is one of the masterpieces of the early sixteenth century, begun *c.* 1500 by Bishop Louis d'Amboise. It contrasts strongly with the simplicity of the general plan.

208. PERPIGNAN   Interior

Another example of the southern type of wide aisleless church. The buttresses are brought
under the roof and enclose side-chapels. The vault is 53 feet in span, and the web between
the ribs is said to be constructed of terra-cotta jars set in concrete, on the old Roman plan.

Begun 1324, but not finished till 1509.

209. NOTRE-DAME-DE-L'ÉPINE (near Chalons-sur-Marne)   Interior

Begun in 1419. The work continued till 1459, after which there was a break, and the western bays and façade were only completed early in the sixteenth century.

This is an example, rare in the Middle Ages, of an archaistic work, the style and general appearance being much more like that of the fourteenth than the fifteenth century.

Note the choir-screen or "jubé", in which the ogee arches alone indicate the later date.

310

210. CAEN   Saint-Jean—interior of nave

Rebuilt after 1417. A good example of Flamboyant architecture in Normandy. The sharply cut arch-mouldings are either carried right down to the ground or interrupted by insignificant capitals. The richly carved balustrade protecting a narrow gangway below the clerestory windows replaces the older triforium, and becomes a striking feature in several churches of this period.

211. Vendôme   La Trinité—nave looking west

This church is of mixed dates, the tower of the twelfth century having been illustrated in
pl. 110 b. The eastern bays of the nave were built in the fourteenth century, and the four
western bays with the façade in the fifteenth. The junction of the work is shown here.
In the later arcade the bases have been raised, the capitals suppressed, and smaller
modifications made in the section of the mouldings. The triforium and clerestory had
already been combined into a single design, and had only to be continued.

212. ROUEN   Saint-Maclou—interior of aisle

Begun in 1437, but not finished till 1541, this church is a striking example of Flamboyant style. The prismatic mouldings carried down to the ground and up to the vault ribs are a thoroughly logical form of construction. For the western porch see pl. 225. The spire has been rebuilt in modern times.

213. Brou   Interior of nave

Built as a family mausoleum by Margaret of Austria, Duchess of Savoy, daughter of the
Emperor Maximilian, this abbey church, which retains its screens, stalls, glass and
magnificently carved altar-pieces and tombs, enables us to picture the ideals of the latest
Gothic period better than any other building.

Margaret, who by that time had been installed as governor of the Low Countries at
Malines, in 1512 sent Loys van Boghem, a Flemish master-mason, to erect the church. It
was finished 1532. Certain Flemish features are very evident, especially in the exterior
where there is a clumsiness of design which we should not have expected from French
masters. In the interior the prismatic mouldings carried right round and the balustrade
under the clerestory are typical. The elaborate bases show the typical outline of Flamboyant
style.

214. Caudebec-en-Caux
From aisle

An inscription states that the nave was begun in 1426, but it is probable that the façade and fine open-work spire were not reached till considerably later.

Here the round columns are retained, but the arch-mouldings are not brought down to the capitals, which consist of a narrow wreath of spikey foliage, but die into the column in a way that is more ingenious than beautiful. Such a design paves the way for the total abolition of the capital, which henceforth has no structural function to perform.

21-2

215. SAINT-RIQUIER   Interior from west

The design of this fine fifteenth-century church was somewhat modified by the retention o
the thirteenth-century arcade of the choir. The whole of the upper part and the nave was
rebuilt *c*. 1457, was damaged by a fire in 1487 and only completed *c*. 1517.

The triforium was abolished and is only represented by a balustrade beneath the lofty
clerestory windows.

The high vaults only date from the seventeenth century, though they probably follow
the original lines of those which collapsed after a fire in 1554. For those of the aisles which
survived see pl. 216 a.

216. (a) SAINT-RIQUIER   Nave aisle   (b) COUTANCES   Saint-Pierre—interior

(a) A rich example of a late vault, with ribs arranged in a star pattern—perhaps suggested by such English vaults as that at Tewkesbury. The nave columns retain the older section of a circle with four minor shafts as they continue the design of the thirteenth-century choir arcade, but there are no capitals on the outer wall, which is entirely in the later style.

(b) An inscription states that the main body of the fabric was finished in 1494, the tower being later. The mouldings merging into round columns, and the plain wall with balustraded passage at the bottom which replace the triforium, produce rather a heavy effect.

317

217. CAEN   Saint-Pierre—interior

The nave was originally built in the fourteenth century, but transformed and vaulted in
the fifteenth or sixteenth. About 1520 the apse was rebuilt in an extravagantly ornate
manner, and the eastern aisles and chapels were constructed on a Gothic plan but with
Renaissance details. Pendant bosses were set in the vaults, and a strange attempt made to
devise tracery and detail in a Classical manner. This can best be seen on the exterior (see
pl. 245).

   The grand spire of *c.* 1308 is shown in pl. 193 b.

218. (a) Gisors   Aisle and chapels   (b) Rouen   Saint-Vincent—porch

(a) A good example of late Flamboyant style, apparently early sixteenth century. Vaulting ribs merge into the pillars without any capitals, and some of the lesser pillars have a spiral panelling.

(b) A fine late fifteenth-century porch, with ogee arch-heads, elaborate cusping and open balustrade.

(a)

(b)

219. (a) TROYES   Sainte-Savine—interior
       (b) CAEN   Saint-Jean—balustrade

(a) A typical church of the Troyes district, built early in the sixteenth century. The nave is not much higher than the aisles and there are no clerestory windows. The vaulting ribs die away into the pillars, and the whole effect is clumsy and rather ugly.

(b) Placed under the clerestory windows. These richly carved balustrades take the place of the triforium, and are an effective feature of a good many fifteenth-century churches.

320

220. VENDÔME   La Trinité—façade

A very fine example of fifteenth-century Flamboyant style. There are no flanking towers,
as the old twelfth-century belfry (pl. 110 b) still stands almost detached at the side. Tracery
replaced sculpture in the tympanum of the doorway, and a lofty open-work pediment is
raised over the arch. The tracery in this, on the wall surface and windows is almost entirely
composed of "mouchettes" (see pp. 71, 72) and their flame-like shapes give a good idea of
how the Flamboyant style got its name. Cusping is carried round arches, even those of the
flying buttresses, and the whole effect is rich and sumptuous, if a little restless.

221. AUXERRE CATHEDRAL   Façade

Begun in the middle of the thirteenth century with the south doorway, progress was slow
and the north lateral doorway seems to belong to *c.* 1300. The sculpture of these doorways,
though mutilated, is particularly charming. The central doorway and most of the front is
fifteenth century, but the upper part of the north tower was only completed by the middle
of the sixteenth. The south tower was never finished.

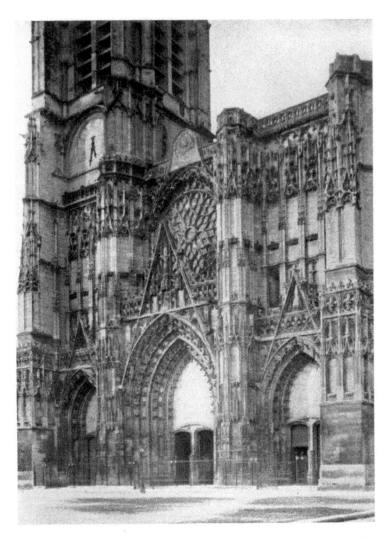

222. TROYES CATHEDRAL   Façade

Begun from plans by the celebrated architect Martin Chambiges in 1507. It was complete
by 1559 with the exception of the upper part of the tower, which was only finished in 1638.
The south tower was never completed. The numerous statues and the reliefs of the tympana
were destroyed at the Revolution, but in spite of this the general effect is rich and stately.

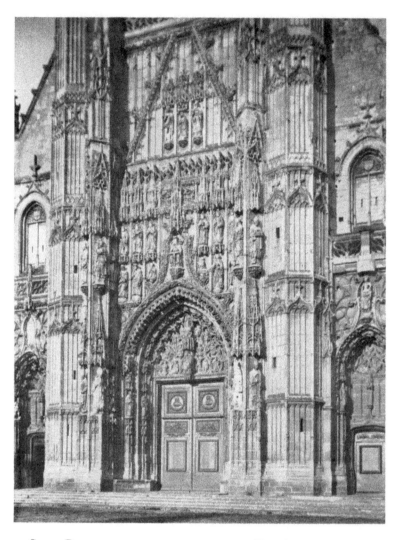

223. Saint-Riquier   Façade and west doorways

Built under Abbot Thibaut de Bayencourt (1511–36), the splendid central doorway serves to give a good idea of the magnificence of the architecture of this period as the bulk of the statuary has survived, though somewhat weather-beaten in places.

224. ROUEN CATHEDRAL   Façade

This is a mixed construction of various dates. The original lateral doorways of the first
quarter of the thirteenth century, and the rose window of 1370, have been incorporated in
the wonderful Flamboyant screen begun in 1509. The towers are placed outside the aisles,
as at Wells, and serve to give great breadth to the façade. The rich open-work screen with
its gables and statues has not proved very resistant to the weather and has necessitated
extensive restorations.

325

225. ROUEN   Saint-Maclou—façade

This magnificent parish church was begun *c.* 1436, and the bulk of it finished *c.* 1480. Final
touches, however, were not made until after 1500. The façade, which has five open porches, bent back
at the sides, is very ornate, with rich sculpture, and open-work balustrades and gables. There is a
somewhat similar façade at Alençon.

226. CLAMEÇY   Façade

An example of a fifteenth-century façade from Burgundy. There are more plain surfaces
than in some of these fronts, but the doorway, gable, niches and buttresses are enriched
with the same profusion of carving as elsewhere. The façade is flanked by a fine early
sixteenth-century tower (see pl. 235 b).

227. ABBEVILLE   Saint-Vulfran—façade

Begun 1480, this church was left unfinished in 1539. In spite of a restoration which has
deprived the sculptured detail of much of its charm, this façade is a magnificent composition,
and as it has all been completed in one style to the original design it is one of the most
satisfactory and picturesque examples in France.

The church behind is only a fragment with an east end rudely patched up in the
seventeenth century.

228. SENS CATHEDRAL   North transept

Transept fronts are sometimes rivals of the west façade. This one was built between 1503 and 1513, and the design is attributed to Martin Chambiges who was also responsible for the west front at Troyes. The doorway has a series of niches for statues instead of reliefs in the tympanum. Note also the elaborate cusping of the arches, the open-work balustrades and the vast rose window filling the whole width between the buttresses and united in one composition with traceried windows which bring it down to the top of the porch.

229. EVREUX CATHEDRAL   North transept

Another extremely rich and effective transept front. The date seems to be *c.* 1500–20, and
the master-mason's name, Jean Cossart, is preserved.

230. SENLIS CATHEDRAL   South transept

In 1504 Senlis was seriously damaged by a fire, and a large part of the upper portions of
the church had to be rebuilt. The transept fronts seem to have been the last work undertaken,
and the south transept was built between 1530 and 1534. One of the master-masons was
Pierre Chambiges, son of the Martin Chambiges who was employed at Troyes, Sens and
Beauvais.

The twisted columns, flattened arches and pendant cusps are marks of the latest types of
Flamboyant.

231. Caudebec   West porches

A rich example of fifteenth-century doorways. Though the general plan of the thirteenth
century survives in the triple doors with statue-lined buttresses between them, all the
details have changed. The statues, now missing, were placed in niches beneath tall and
elaborate canopies, like those of the wooden stalls, sharply-cut foliage runs round the arch-
moulds between the figures, and above the top of the arches are the ogee pediments and
lace-like panelling of the regular Flamboyant type.

232. LOUVIERS   South porch

One of the most elaborate pieces of Flamboyant design in existence. The tall ogee canopies of pierced stone-work and crocketed niches are carried along the whole southern face of the nave-aisle, and over the porch are of a most intricate design. The heavy pendant suspended over the void in the centre of the doubled arch over the doorway is a clever trick typical of the way in which masons of this period liked to exhibit their brilliant technique.

Date—late fifteenth century.

233. ALBI CATHEDRAL   South porch

This porch seems to have been planned in connexion with the other enrichments initiated by Bishop Louis d'Amboise, but was not carried out during his lifetime. It is dated 1519–35. The wealth of detail is in astonishing contrast with the plain brick fortress walls of the cathedral. The return to the round arch is a sign of the coming change to Italian forms.

234. (a) CHAUMONT   South porch   (b) RODEZ CATHEDRAL   Tower

a) Two doorways on the south side of this church are typical examples of the "Rayonnant" style of the fourteenth century and the Flamboyant of the fifteenth and sixteenth. The later and smaller one is shown in pl. 241 a.

b) This great tower, 285 feet high, is the pride of the Rouergue. The lower stages date from the late fourteenth century, but the upper part from 1510 to 1526. An octagonal lantern takes the place of a spire.

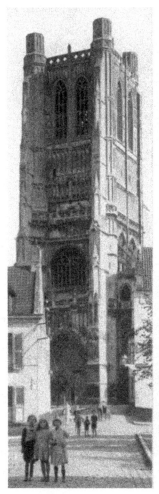 

235. (a) SAINT-OMER   (b) CLAMEÇY   Tower
       Tour Saint-Bertin

(a) This fine tower stands over the west door of the ruined abbey of Saint-Bertin. It was begun in the fifteenth century and finished *c.* 1520. It is finished off with a flat platform with pinnacles at the corners, and English influence has been suggested, but these features are too common in the picturesque towers of this period for this point to be insisted on.

(b) This single tower stands at the side of the façade and may be taken as representing the Flamboyant towers of north-eastern France and Burgundy. The first stone was laid in 1497.

336

236. ROUEN   Saint-Ouen—tower

This very picturesque central tower dates from the end of the fifteenth and beginning of the sixteenth centuries. It is possible that it was intended to carry up the crowning octagon as a spire, but that this was abandoned from considerations of prudence.

237. NOTRE-DAME-DE-L'ÉPINE (near Chalons-sur-Marne)   Façade

This very striking twin-spired façade was added to the rather earlier church (see pl. 209) early in the sixteenth century, and in spite of restoration presents a most imposing appearance. The open-work spires with little flying buttresses and crockets are good examples of this last phase of Gothic design, and the difference between them prevents the too rigid symmetry which French Flamboyant builders disliked.

238. Soissons   Saint-Jean-des-Vignes—façade

This grand façade belongs to a church which has long ago disappeared, and has itself
suffered cruel mutilations both in the war of 1870 and in the Great War. This photograph
was taken before the more recent of these disasters, when considerable portions of the
spires were knocked down by German shells.

The lower part of the façade and doorways is work of the middle, or second half, of the
thirteenth century, but the towers and spires date from the opening years of the sixteenth
century, the last stone having been placed in 1520.

339

239. (a) Lisieux   Lady Chapel   (b) Caudebec   Choi

Examples of Flamboyant window tracery. In the east window at Lisieux the tracery is twisted abou
in a most uncomfortable manner. That at Caudebec is more satisfactory, but is inferior to that of th
English Decorated style, from which some authorities think it is derived, and lacks the dignity of ou
sober contemporary Perpendicular.

 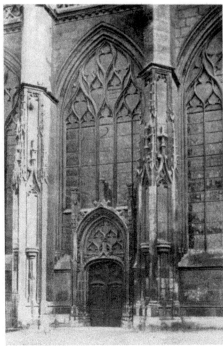

240. (a) LE MANS CATHEDRAL   (b) ROUEN
　　　　　 North transept   Saint-Ouen—windows of nave aisle

(a) Built 1403-30. The enormous windows are filled with a complicated tracery scheme, but it has not yet quite reached the typical Flamboyant forms, and in that on the left especially retains something of the "Rayonnant" or Geometric style.

(b) The nave was not finished till the time of Abbot Bohier, 1491-1515, but is a good example of fifteenth-century style. The tracery of the windows is mainly made up of ogee arches and the shapes called "soufflets" and "mouchettes" (see p. 72).

241. (a) CHAUMONT   (b) RUE
        Door on south side   Vault of Chapelle du Saint-Esprit

(a) A typical fifteenth-century Flamboyant doorway on a small scale. Note the ogee containing arch and deep mouldings filled with undercut spikey foliage.

(b) An example of the extreme elaboration reached in small vaults at the end of the fifteenth or beginning of the sixteenth century. Multiplication of ribs arranged to form star patterns, large pendants and everything covered with foliage and tracery patterns give this little chapel a character of extreme richness.

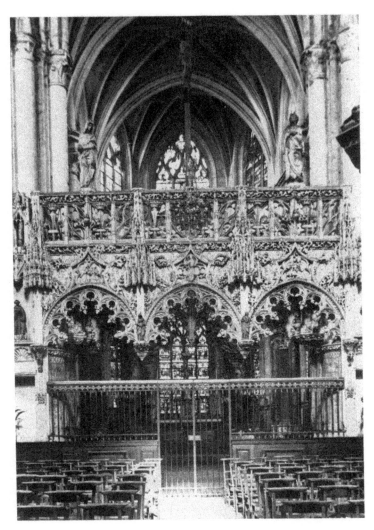

242. Troyes   La Madeleine—jubé

An example of the rich interior fittings of the latest Gothic period. These choir-screens
(or jubés) are more common in Flanders than in France proper, but relations between the
two were close at this time. This elaborate construction, with the central arch apparently
suspended in the air without supports, was the masterpiece of the master-mason Jean
Gualde who made it during the years 1508–17. On his tomb-slab originally placed beneath
it was an inscription that he waited for the resurrection in that place without fear of being
crushed.

243. RUE   Flamboyant carvin

A good example of the sharply undercut foliage and crisp leafage of *c.* 1500.

344

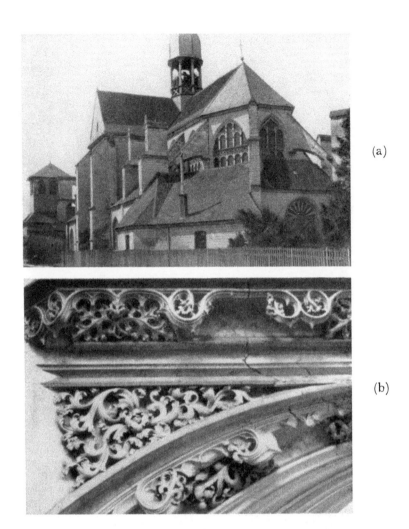

(a)

(b)

244. (a) TROYES   Saint-Martin
     (b) BROU   Foliage of window to oratory of Margaret of Austria

(a) This extremely ugly church was begun *c.* 1590 and was a long time building. It is interesting as showing how long the traditions of the old Gothic plan were retained with its vault and flying buttresses. The attempt to invent a Classical type of tracery is curious rather than beautiful.

(b) A good example of the sharp undercut foliage, based on the thistle rather than the vine or acanthus, typical of the finest work of the Flemish masons working under Van Boghem in the first quarter of the sixteenth century.

345

245. CAEN   Saint-Pierre—apse chapels

One of the richest examples of the attempt to adapt Renaissance details to a Gothic plan.
The windows are round-headed, with curious ungraceful tracery, and pinnacles copied
from Classical urns or candelabra.
    Date *c.* 1520.

INDEXES

INDEX TO TEXT

GG
349
23

INDEX TO TEXT

INDEX TO PLATES

The figures refer to plate numbers

Milton Keynes UK
Ingram Content Group UK Ltd.
UKHW051157150424
441157UK00001B/2